The Crucial
Elements
of the Bible

The
Holy
Word
for
Morning
Revival

Witness Lee

Living Stream Ministry
Anaheim, CA • www.lsm.org

First Edition, June 2011.

ISBN 978-0-7363-4818-8

Published by

Living Stream Ministry
2431 W. La Palma Ave., Anaheim, CA 92801 U.S.A.
P. O. Box 2121, Anaheim, CA 92814 U.S.A.

Printed in the United States of America

11 12 13 / 4 3 2 1

Contents

Preface

1. This book is intended as an aid to believers in developing a daily time of morning revival with the Lord in His word. At the same time, it provides a limited review of the Memorial Day weekend conference held in Dallas, Texas, May 27-30, 2011. The general subject of the conference was "The Crucial Elements of the Bible." Through intimate contact with the Lord in His word, the believers can be constituted with life and truth and thereby equipped to prophesy in the meetings of the church unto the building up of the Body of Christ.

2. The entire content of this book is taken primarily from the published conference outlines, the text and footnotes of the Recovery Version of the Bible, selections from the writings of Witness Lee and Watchman Nee, and *Hymns,* all of which are published by Living Stream Ministry.

3. The book is divided into weeks. One conference message is covered per week. Each week presents first the message outline, followed by six daily portions, a hymn, and then some space for writing. The message outline has been divided into days, corresponding to the six daily portions. Each daily portion covers certain points and begins with a section entitled "Morning Nourishment." This section contains selected verses and a short reading that can provide rich spiritual nourishment through intimate fellowship with the Lord. The "Morning Nourishment" is followed by a section entitled "Today's Reading," a longer portion of ministry related to the day's main points. Each day's portion concludes with a short list of references for further reading and some space for the saints to make notes concerning their spiritual inspiration, enlightenment, and enjoyment to serve as a reminder of what they have received of the Lord that day.

4. The space provided at the end of each week is for composing a short prophecy. This prophecy can be composed by considering all of our daily notes, the "harvest" of our

inspirations during the week, and preparing a main point with some sub-points to be spoken in the church meetings for the organic building up of the Body of Christ.

5. Following the last week in this volume, we have provided reading schedules for both the Old and New Testaments in the Recovery Version with footnotes. These schedules are arranged so that one can read through both the Old and New Testaments of the Recovery Version with footnotes in two years.

6. As a practical aid to the saints' feeding on the Word throughout the day, we have provided verse cards at the end of the volume, which correspond to each day's scripture reading. These may be removed and carried along as a source of spiritual enlightenment and nourishment in the saints' daily lives.

7. The conference message outlines were compiled by Living Stream Ministry from the writings of Witness Lee and Watchman Nee. The outlines, footnotes, and references in the Recovery Version of the Bible are by Witness Lee. All of the other references cited in this publication are from the published ministry of Witness Lee and Watchman Nee.

Memorial Day Weekend Conference
(May 27-30, 2011)

General Subject:

The Crucial Elements of the Bible

Banners:

Christ, the Spirit, life, and the church
are the crucial elements of the Bible, and
a principle that we must apply
in our interpretation of the Bible
is Christ, the Spirit, life, and the church.

M1

The Gospel of John reveals that Christ became flesh
to be the Lamb of God to accomplish redemption
and that in resurrection He became
the life-giving Spirit, another Comforter,
to breathe Himself into the believers.

M3

Through and in His resurrection Christ
as the last Adam became the life-giving Spirit
to enter into His believers to flow out
as rivers of living water.

The Body of Christ as the axis of God's economy
is not an organization manufactured by man
but an organism produced by the Triune God as life.

M6

The Crucial Elements of the Bible— Christ, the Spirit, Life, and the Church

Scripture Reading: Matt. 16:16, 18; John 3:15; Rom. 8:2; Eph. 1:22-23; 4:4-6

Day 1

I. **Christ, the Spirit, life, and the church are the crucial elements of the Bible (Matt. 16:16, 18; John 20:31; 7:39; Rom. 8:11; Col. 3:4; Eph. 1:22-23):**
   A. Christ, the Spirit, life, and the church are the contents of the Bible.
   B. A principle that we must apply in our interpretation of the Bible is Christ, the Spirit, life, and the church (Rom. 9:5; 8:2, 11; 12:4-5; 16:1, 4-5, 16b).

Day 2

II. **Christ, the Spirit, life, and the church are the extracts of the Bible:**
   A. With Christ the emphasis is that Christ is the believers' life and is united and mingled with the believers (Col. 3:4; John 15:4-5; 1 Cor. 6:17):
      1. In addition to knowing Christ as the Savior and the Redeemer, we need to know Him in a deeper way—that He is our life and that He is in us to be united and mingled with us (Col. 3:4; 1:27; John 15:4-5).
      2. Because the Lord is the Spirit, we can abide in Him and the Lord can abide in us; we coinhere with the Lord; that is, we are in Him and He is in us (2 Cor. 3:17a; John 14:20; 17:21).
      3. Our being united and mingled with the Lord can take place only in our regenerated spirit; hence, this mingling results in our being joined to the Lord as one spirit (1 Cor. 6:17).
      4. Christ is our life and our person, and He is united and mingled with us; He is also working in us to transform us until we are the same as He is in life, nature, and expression but not in the Godhead (2 Cor. 3:18).
      5. He and we are one; He is the Head of the

Body, and we are the members of the Body (1 Cor. 12:12-13; Eph. 1:22-23).

6. "O what a miracle, my Lord, / That I'm in Thee and Thou in me, / That Thou and I are really one; / O what a wondrous mystery!" (*Hymns,* #233).

Day 3

Aptos

B. With the Spirit the emphasis is that the Holy Spirit of God has been compounded with Christ's divinity, humanity, crucifixion, and resurrection to be the compound, life-giving, indwelling, sanctifying, transforming, and sevenfold intensified Spirit (Exo. 30:23-25; 1 Cor. 15:45b; Rom. 8:11; 15:16b; 2 Cor. 3:18; Rev. 4:5):

1. The Spirit is the consummation of the Triune God after passing through various processes; in the Spirit there are the elements of the Father, the Son, and the Spirit (Matt. 1:18, 20; Luke 1:35; Heb. 9:14; Rom. 8:11).

2. Today the Spirit is the compound Spirit (Exo. 30:23-25), compounded with the Spirit of God and Christ's two natures—the divine nature and the human nature—with His death and resurrection to be the compound, life-giving (1 Cor. 15:45b), indwelling (Rom. 8:11), sanctifying (15:16b), and transforming Spirit (2 Cor. 3:18).

3. Such a Spirit has the bountiful supply and even is the bountiful supply for our experience and enjoyment (Phil. 1:19).

4. Economically, the compound Spirit has become the seven Spirits of God to supply us in a sevenfold intensified way so that we may accomplish God's economy concerning the church in this age of degradation (Rev. 1:4; 3:1; 4:5; 5:6).

Day 4

Woords

C. With life the emphasis is that God in Christ as the Spirit of reality is the believers' life so that they may live Him out as the processed Triune God (1 Cor. 1:30; John 14:17; Phil. 1:19-21a):

1. Life is the Spirit, who is the Triune God Himself, and life is Christ (Rom. 8:2; John 11:25; 14:6; Col. 3:4).

2. God has given to us eternal life, and this life is in His Son; if we have the Son, we have the life (1 John 5:11-12).

3. God in Christ has passed through His various processes and was consummated as the Spirit; now as the Spirit of reality He is life to the believers so that they may live Him out as the processed Triune God (John 7:39; 14:17, 19b).

4. When we believed in Christ, the Son of God, He came into us to be our life and person and to live and move with us (3:15-16; Gal. 2:20).

Day 5

D. With the church the emphasis is that the believers are on the ground of oneness to be the testimony of the Body of Christ (Eph. 1:23; 4:1-6):

1. The church is composed of a group of people who have been called out of the world by God; God has called us out of every tribe, tongue, people, and nation and has gathered us together to be the church (Matt. 16:18; 18:17; Rev. 5:9; 7:9).

2. As believers in Christ, we have been begotten of God with His life and we have the divine life within us; we have been regenerated to become people of the kingdom of the heavens and brothers and sisters in His universal family (John 1:12-13; 3:3, 5, 15; Eph. 2:19).

3. The church is an entity of life, an organism, with a life and person; this life and person are the Triune God Himself, who is the element of the oneness of the church (4:3-6).

4. The universal Body of Christ is expressed as local churches; the ground of the church is the oneness of the Body of Christ (1 Cor. 12:12-13, 27; 1:2; Eph. 1:23; 4:3-6).

Day 6

5. We were all baptized into one Body, and we all have one Spirit, one Lord, and one God and

Father; now we must stand on the ground of oneness to be the unique testimony of the Body of Christ and to live the practical church life (1 Cor. 12:13; Eph. 4:4-6; Rev. 1:11).

III. **We must develop any biblical truth in the way of Christ, the Spirit, life, and the church (2 Tim. 2:15):**

A. Any message or development of the truth in the Bible without Christ, the Spirit, life, and the church is an empty shell with no content (1 Tim. 1:6-7).

B. It is always safe to develop a biblical truth in the way of Christ, the Spirit, life, and the church; for example, we should develop the truth concerning holiness with Christ, the Spirit, life, and the church (1 Cor. 1:30; Rom. 6:22; Eph. 5:26).

Morning Nourishment

Rom. And if the Spirit of the One who raised Jesus from
8:11 the dead dwells in you, He who raised Christ from the
dead will also give life to your mortal bodies through
His Spirit who indwells you.

Eph. And He subjected all things under His feet and gave
1:22-23 Him *to be* Head over all things to the church, which is
His Body, the fullness of the One who fills all in all.

The Bible was written by men under God's inspiration. Compared to God, man is simple; hence, the way that the Bible was written is also simple. In particular, the Bible presents the divine and mystical matters in a way that is easily understandable to us. For this reason, the Bible seems to contain some "bark" and "branches." In their reading of the Bible, many Christians often touch only these superficial things. They do not penetrate the Bible to touch its kernel. They do not touch the spirit and life in the depths of the Bible nor know the real, crucial elements in it. We must go beyond the superficial branches and bark and enter into the depths of the Bible in order to touch its spirit, its kernel, and to know its crucial elements. (*The Four Crucial Elements of the Bible—Christ, the Spirit, Life, and the Church,* p. 8)

Today's Reading

A nut consists of a shell, the meat, and the kernel, which is the center. Man is also of three parts: the outer part—the physical organs; the inner part—the soul; and the innermost part—the spirit (1 Thes. 5:23). Of these three parts—spirit, soul, and body—the most important part is the innermost part, the spirit, which is the breath of life in man (Gen. 2:7). Without such a breath of life, it is not possible for man to exist, and man thus ceases to be man. Likewise, the Bible has its kernel, its life, its center, which is constituted with the church, Christ, the Spirit, and life. These four items are the contents of the true substance of the Bible....These four crucial elements are also the four important items in the Lord's recovery today. Hence, we must all have a deep impression, a fresh light, and a renewed understanding concerning these four crucial elements.

We all must clearly see these four crucial elements—the church, Christ, the Spirit, and life. The church is a group of people with the Triune God, having His life. Christ is our Savior and Redeemer, who has come into us to be our life and to be united and mingled with us. The Spirit as the consummation of the processed Triune God comes into us to be our reality. When we have Him, we have Christ's divine nature and human nature, and we also have Christ's incarnation, human living, crucifixion, resurrection, and ascension. Such a One is now in us as our life. (*The Four Crucial Elements of the Bible—Christ, the Spirit, Life, and the Church*, pp. 8, 15)

Any message or any development of the Bible without Christ, the Spirit, life, and the church is an empty shell with no content. The content of the Bible is Christ, the Spirit, life, and the church. At least one of these items must be present in your development of the truth. Also, in your preaching of the gospel at least one of these items should be present. I saw some evangelists in China who preached quite prevailingly, but in their gospel they did not preach much reality of Christ, the Spirit, life, and the church. Their prevailing evangelical work attracted a good number of people. However, many of these people turned to the way of the Lord's recovery to pick up Christ, the Spirit, life, and the church. They all remained and became very useful to the Lord's interest. Those who did not turn this way, including the evangelists, either disappeared or still remained with emptiness. In their gospel campaigns a number were saved, but after ten years many disappeared or remained empty. We must thank the Lord, however, that many also turned this way. The ones who turned this way not only remained but they became solid with the truth concerning Christ, the Spirit, life, and the church. (*Elders' Training, Book 3: The Way to Carry Out the Vision*, pp. 63-64)

Further Reading: The Crucial Points of the Major Items of the Lord's Recovery Today; The Basic Revelation in the Holy Scriptures, chs. 1-5

Enlightenment and inspiration: _____

_____

_____

_____

Morning Nourishment

Col. When Christ our life is manifested, then you also
3:4   will be manifested with Him in glory.
1 Cor. But he who is joined to the Lord is one spirit.
6:17

When I first went to Taiwan, I studied the Bible with the brothers and sisters every day. In one year we studied sixty topics, which are the sixty topics in *Crucial Truths in the Holy Scriptures*. However, after studying that many topics, eventually I have to admit that the extracts of the Bible are nothing other than these four items: Christ, the Spirit, life, and the church. In the beginning is Christ, at the end is the church, and in the process are the Spirit and life....Everything spoken of in the Bible is for these four items. Only Christ is the reality; He is the body of all things (Col. 2:17). If there is no Christ, there is no Spirit, and neither are there life and the church. If there is Christ, there is reality and substance. Christ is the Spirit, the Spirit is life, and life produces the church. Without Christ, there is no Spirit; without the Spirit, there is no life; and without life, there is no way to produce the church. Hence, these four items are the extract, the cream, the essence, of the Bible. (*The Four Crucial Elements of the Bible—Christ, the Spirit, Life, and the Church*, p. 37)

Today's Reading

[A] crucial element of the Bible is Christ. Generally, the initial knowledge of Christians concerning Christ is that He is the Savior (Luke 2:11), the One who is full of love and compassion to save them from hell. After a little reading of the Bible, they may know Him further as the Redeemer (Matt. 20:28), who died and shed His blood on the cross as a ransom for many to satisfy God's righteous requirements (1 Pet. 1:18-19; Rev. 1:5b). However, it is not enough to know Christ only to this extent. In addition to knowing Christ as the Savior and Redeemer, we must know Him to a deeper degree, that is, that He is our life and He is also in us to be united and mingled with us. In

John 15:5 the Lord Jesus said, "I am the vine; you are the branches. He who abides in Me and I in him, he bears much fruit." It is a mystery that we abide in the Lord and He abides in us. It is difficult for human language to describe this mysterious union. Just as we abide in the air, and the air also abides in us, today because the Lord is the Spirit, we can abide in the Lord and the Lord can also abide in us. What a miracle! What a mystery! The Lord abides in us and is united and mingled with us! Stanza 1 of *Hymns,* #233 says, "O what a miracle, my Lord, / That I'm in Thee and Thou in me, / That Thou and I are really one; / O what a wondrous mystery!"

The Bible clearly reveals that the Triune God not only coexists but also coinheres; the Son is in the Father and the Father is in the Son (John 14:10-11). Likewise, we also coinhere with the Lord; we abide in the Lord, and the Lord abides in us (v. 20; 17:21). This is the mingling of the Lord with us. This is a matter not only *of* the divine life but also *in* the divine life. Our being united and mingled with the Lord can transpire only in our spirit. Hence, this mingling results in our being joined to the Lord as one spirit (1 Cor. 6:17). We need to know Christ to such an extent. Eventually, He becomes us and we become Him—He and we are one. He is the Head of the Body, and we are the members of the Body (1 Cor. 12:12-13; Eph. 1:22-23). After His resurrection Christ ascended to the heavens and sat down on the right hand of God (Heb. 1:3; 10:12). Moreover, today He is also the Spirit dwelling in us. He is our life (Col. 3:4a) and our person and is always united and mingled with us. He is also working in us to transform us until He becomes us and we become Him (2 Cor. 3:18). This is the Christ revealed in the holy Word. (*The Four Crucial Elements of the Bible—Christ, the Spirit, Life, and the Church,* pp. 11-12)

Further Reading: Ten Lines in the Bible, ch. 2; *The Central Thought of God,* chs. 1-2; *Vital Factors for the Recovery of the Church Life,* ch. 1

Enlightenment and inspiration: _____

_____

_____

_____

Morning Nourishment

Luke   And the angel answered and said to her, The Holy
1:35   Spirit will come upon you, and the power of the Most
       High will overshadow you; therefore also the holy
       thing which is born will be called the Son of God.
Phil. For I know that for me this will turn out to salvation
1:19   through your petition and *the* bountiful supply of the
       Spirit of Jesus Christ.

[Another] crucial element revealed in the Bible is the Spirit. Traditional Christianity holds an inaccurate concept concerning the Holy Spirit, considering the Holy Spirit merely to be a power or an inspiring force. It was not until the nineteenth century… that some went further to see that the Holy Spirit is not merely a power but God Himself. In the Lord's recovery, after many years of studying the Bible, we have seen clearly that the Spirit is the consummation of the Triune God after passing through various processes. Therefore, in the Spirit there are the elements of the Father, the Son, and the Spirit. (*The Four Crucial Elements of the Bible—Christ, the Spirit, Life, and the Church*, p. 12)

Today's Reading

The holy anointing ointment in Exodus 30:23-25 typifies the Triune God being processed and eventually consummated as the Spirit. The holy anointing ointment…was compounded with a number of elements.…The olive oil and the four kinds of spices added to it were mingled together and compounded to become the holy anointing ointment for the anointing of the tabernacle and all its furniture so that the tabernacle with all its furniture might become most holy, fit to be God's dwelling place.

In the Bible, olive oil typifies the Spirit of God, God Himself. The four kinds of spices signify humanity in God's creation, and oil signifies divinity in the Godhead. Four kinds of spices being mingled with the olive oil to become the holy anointing ointment indicates that the Spirit of God does not merely possess divinity but has been mingled with certain elements.…It was not until the Lord Jesus was glorified in His resurrection (Luke 24:26) that the Holy Spirit became the Spirit of the incarnated, crucified, resurrected, and life-giving Jesus Christ, having both the divine element and the human element, including Christ's divinity and humanity with all the essences and realities of His incarnation, human living, crucifixion, and resurrection. All these items were compounded in this Spirit. Hence, this Spirit is now the flowing, living water for us to receive.

The Spirit was ultimately consummated by Christ through His processes. As God in eternity with divinity, Christ became a man with humanity and lived the human life on earth for thirty-three and a half years. Then He entered into death, came out of death in resurrection, and ascended to the heavens. These are the processes that He passed through. By passing through all these processes, He became the consummated life-giving Spirit (1 Cor. 15:45b). We may illustrate the compound Spirit with a beverage that is a compound of water with honey, lemon, tea, and salt. When we drink this beverage, we take in not only the water but also the honey, lemon, tea, and salt. Likewise, today the Spirit is the compound Spirit, compounded with the Holy Spirit of God and Christ's two natures—the divine nature and the human nature—with His death and resurrection to be the compound, life-giving, indwelling (Rom. 8:11), sanctifying (15:16b), and transforming (2 Cor. 3:18) Spirit. Such a Spirit has the bountiful supply and even is the bountiful supply for our experience and enjoyment (Phil. 1:19). Eventually, this compound Spirit has even become the seven Spirits of God to supply us in a sevenfold intensified way that we may accomplish God's divine economy concerning the church in this age of degradation (Rev. 1:4; 4:5; 5:6). Today the Triune God is in the church as a person, and Christ is in the believers as a person. The Triune God as a person in the church and Christ as a person in the believers are nothing less than the Spirit. Hallelujah, we have such an all-inclusive Spirit! (*The Four Crucial Elements of the Bible—Christ, the Spirit, Life, and the Church*, pp. 12-14)

Further Reading: The Spirit and the Body, chs. 2-8

Enlightenment and inspiration: _____

_____

_____

_____

Morning Nourishment

John   *Even* the Spirit of reality...you know Him, because He
14:17 abides with you and shall be in you.
 Gal.   I am crucified with Christ; and *it is* no longer I *who*
 2:20 live, but *it is* Christ *who* lives in me; and the *life* which
       I now live in the flesh I live in faith, the *faith* of the Son
       of God, who loved me and gave Himself up for me.

[Another] crucial element revealed in the Bible is life. Life is
the Spirit, of whom we have spoken previously and who is the Triune God Himself. Furthermore, this life is also Christ. God in
Christ passed through His various processes and was consummated as the Spirit. Now as the Spirit of reality (John 14:17) He is
life to the believers that they may live Him out as the processed
Triune God. When we believe in the Lord, this Lord in whom we
believe immediately comes into us to be our life and person and to
live and move with us. Once we believe in the Lord and receive
Him, He also expects us to hand ourselves over to Him. Hence, as
the Lord and we receive one another, He and we are mingled with
one another. (*The Four Crucial Elements of the Bible—Christ, the
Spirit, Life, and the Church,* p. 14)

Today's Reading

Before we were saved, we were alone in ourselves, but after
being saved we are no longer merely ourselves but are united and
mingled with the Lord as one. This may be likened to a married
life. Before a person is married, he is alone, but after he is married, he is no longer one person living alone but two persons living
together. However, a couple living together is an outward matter;
the Lord Jesus and we live together by being united and mingled
as one. Hence, this is a great mystery (Eph. 5:31-32).

Concerning our living today, we should be able to say as Paul
said, "I am crucified with Christ; and it is no longer I who live, but
it is Christ who lives in me; and the life which I now live in the flesh
I live in faith, the faith of the Son of God" (Gal. 2:20). The life we
live today is not a life we live by our natural old man. Instead, it is
a life we live by faith, a life we live by believing that the invisible

Triune God is in us as our person and our life so that we may become members of the church as the Body of Christ, coordinating with all the saints on the ground of oneness as the testimony of the oneness of the Body of Christ. (*The Four Crucial Elements of the Bible—Christ, the Spirit, Life, and the Church,* pp. 14-15)

The Lord Jesus—the great God who is inside of us, who has become our life, who has put us on, and who is joined with us—should be the One who is living and doing. Our living must be His living, our speaking must be His speaking, and our moving must be His moving.

The Gospel of John has twenty-one chapters. Together these chapters reveal that the eternal God became flesh to be the Lamb of God to accomplish redemption on our behalf. This entire Gospel also unveils that after this God entered into death, He came out of death and was transfigured to be the life-giving Spirit to enter into our spirit to live and move with us. In light of this we should consecrate ourselves to Him, stopping all of our own living and moving, and open up to Him by calling on His name, eating His word, and contacting Him, so that He can supply us and cause us to walk in newness of life. The Lord desires to gain such a group of people on the earth today. By living in this way we will not only have been regenerated and redeemed, we will also be in the process of being transformed. Day after day He will change our nature into His very nature and conform us into His very image. Then one day He will bring us into glory and all of us will be built up together to be His exceedingly glorious expression.

May our eyes be opened to see this one matter, and may we open our heart and spirit to Him and say, "Lord, I stop everything. You are not only my life, You are also my living. May my inner being contact You moment by moment and constantly receive Your supply, so that in my daily living You and I will live as one entity." (*Living with the Lord,* pp. 14-16)

Further Reading: Basic Principles of the Experience of Life, chs. 1-2; *Vital Factors for the Recovery of the Church Life,* chs. 2-3

Enlightenment and inspiration: _____

_____

_____

_____

Morning Nourishment

Eph. Being diligent to keep the oneness of the Spirit in the
4:3-6 uniting bond of peace: one Body and one Spirit, even
as also you were called in one hope of your calling;
one Lord, one faith, one baptism; one God and Father
of all, who is over all and through all and in all.

We must have a normal Christian life before we can have a
proper church life. Just as there cannot be a good country without
good citizens, there is no way to produce a good church without
good Christians. Christ is the Spirit, the Spirit is life, and life
issues in the church. (*The Four Crucial Elements of the Bible—
Christ, the Spirit, Life, and the Church*, p. 133)

Today's Reading

[Another] crucial element of the Bible is the church. The
Greek word for *church* is *ekklesia,* which is composed of two
words: *ek,* meaning "out of," and *kaleo,* meaning "call." Hence, in
Greek, the word for *church* means the called-out ones. The early
translators of the Chinese Bible rendered this word as *a religious
assembly*. This term fits man's natural thought, but it spoils the
original meaning. *Ekklesia* does not denote a religious assembly;
it refers to a called-out congregation. Therefore, the most precise
rendering is *assembly*. We are a group of people called out by God;
we are the church.

God has called us out of the world, out of every nation, tribe,
people, and tongue (Rev. 7:9) and has gathered us together to be
the church. Today, regardless of our nationality or race, we have
been called to become the people of the kingdom of the heavens.
Hence, we have the heavenly citizenship. An American of Chinese descent is Chinese according to birth, but he becomes an
American citizen by naturalization. Today we have become the
people of the kingdom of the heavens by "naturalization," by
being called by God, and also by birth, by being regenerated by
God. God not only has called us but also has regenerated us with
His life. We were not adopted by God; we were begotten of Him
with His life. We all have God's divine life in us, and we are

brothers and sisters of one another because we have been born of the same Father. Regardless of our color, race, or nationality, God has called us and regenerated us that we may become people of the kingdom of the heavens and brothers and sisters in His universal family. This is the church.

God's life is God Himself. Therefore, when God regenerates us with His life, He begets us with Himself. Furthermore, He is within us today. The church is an entity of life, and as such, it has a life and a person. The church is not an organization; it is a life entity, an organism, with a life and a person. This life and this person are the Triune God Himself. He is the element of the oneness of the church (Eph. 4:1-6); hence, the church cannot be divided. Since we all have one God, one life, and one person, there is no factor that can divide us.

Since we have the Triune God in us as our life and person, we must live and walk by Him in our daily life (Gal. 5:25) and grow up in all things into Him, who is the Head (Eph. 4:15). It is difficult for husbands and wives not to quarrel in their married life. By the Lord's grace, I have been with my wife for close to thirty years, and although I dare not say that we have never disagreed, I can say that I have never quarreled with her. This is because I have another person in me, the heavenly God Himself who is my person. When I am displeased or unhappy and try to speak something unpleasant, this person who is in me says, "You may speak, but I won't speak; you may go to quarrel, but I won't go." Thus, I can only say, "Lord, if You won't go, then I won't go either." Then the Lord may say, "Wonderful! Since you won't go, stay here and I will be with you." In this way I have a sweet fellowship with the Lord. Instead of quarreling, there is only prayer, the prayer of two persons praying together. I pray and He prays with me; He prays in my prayer. What an enjoyment this is! This is to live and walk by the person in us. (*The Four Crucial Elements of the Bible— Christ, the Spirit, Life, and the Church,* pp. 8-10)

Further Reading: The Spirit and the Body, chs. 12-20

Enlightenment and inspiration: _____

_____

_____

_____

Morning Nourishment

1 Tim. ...Charge certain ones not to teach different things...
1:3-4, 6 which produce questionings rather than God's econ-
       omy, which is in faith...from which things some, hav-
       ing misaimed, have turned aside to vain talking.
2 Tim. Be diligent to present yourself approved to God, an
2:15   unashamed workman, cutting straight the word of
       the truth.

According to what we are naturally, we are from different coun-
tries and different races. We may even be enemies of one another
because of our cultural backgrounds or for historical reasons.
However, in the church life all enmities have been resolved....We
all have one life and one person through regeneration. We have all
been born of the heavenly Father; therefore, we are one. This is a
characteristic of the church. In the church there are no differences
among colors or races, and neither is there any separation due to
language or culture. We have all become one in Christ. We were
all baptized into one Body, and we all have one Spirit, one Lord,
and one God and Father (1 Cor. 12:13; Eph. 4:4-6). Now we must
stand on the ground of oneness in each locality to be the unique
testimony of the Body of Christ and live the practical church life.
(*The Four Crucial Elements of the Bible—Christ, the Spirit, Life,
and the Church,* p. 10)

Today's Reading

Some evangelists preach with eloquent illustrations to attract
people to stir up their interest, but after being interested, all that
is left with them is a good story. Many are merely eloquent speak-
ers with very little Christ. Based upon this principle, we should
check today's preaching. How much Christ, the Spirit, life, and the
church is in today's preaching of the Word? This shows us the
emptiness of today's preaching and teaching. You should not
develop the truth in the Bible in this way, in an empty way. You
must develop the biblical truth in the way of Christ, the Spirit,
life, and the church. Even if you have a good portion of the Word
with a good idea to stir up people's interest, you must consider

whether or not Christ, the Spirit, life, and the church are the content of your message. If they are not the content, you should forget about it. Do not go further to develop anything apart from this governing principle because you will waste your time. Also, you will have no safeguard and you will be led astray.

All the heresies came in by the way of developing the truth in the Bible apart from Christ, the Spirit, life, and the church. Any doctrine developed apart from these four items will issue in heresy or division....Some even developed the doctrine of holiness apart from Christ, the Spirit, life, and the church. We, however, should develop the doctrine of holiness with Christ for the church. We need to tell people that holiness is Christ Himself, and this Christ today is the life-giving Spirit (1 Cor. 15:45)...who imparts the divine life into us for our sanctification. Holiness is God's nature and is related to life. If you do not have God's life, you do not have God's nature, which is holiness. If God's holiness is going to be increased within you, you must live according to God's nature and by God's life. We must also realize that this holy life should not only be for our personal living, but it must also be a part of the church life. If we would develop the doctrine of holiness with Christ, with the Spirit, with life, and with the church, we would see a marvelous revelation. Otherwise, a holiness sect will be created. This is why some have established holiness churches. These are actually holiness divisions cutting the Body into pieces.

It is dangerous to develop any biblical doctrine apart from Christ, the Spirit, life, and the church....Your doctrine...may not be wrong, but eventually the issue of your practice will be a division. It is always safe to develop any doctrine in the Bible with Christ, the Spirit, life, and the church,...[but] never develop [anything] apart from Christ, the Spirit, life, and the church. (*Elders' Training, Book 3: The Way to Carry Out the Vision*, pp. 64-65)

Further Reading: The Four Crucial Elements of the Bible—Christ, the Spirit, Life, and the Church, ch. 1; Elders' Training, Book 3: The Way to Carry Out the Vision, ch. 6

Enlightenment and inspiration: _____

_____

_____

_____

Hymns, #233

1   O what a miracle, my Lord,
That I'm in Thee and Thou in me,
That Thou and I are really one;
O what a wondrous mystery!

2   For me Thy body Thou didst give,
That I may ever share in Thee;
For me Thy precious blood was shed,
That from my sins I might be free.

3   By resurrection Thou didst change
Thy form and as the Spirit come;
Thou wouldst that I be filled with Thee
That all Thy riches mine become.

4   Now as the symbols we behold,
Thy loving self we see anew;
We thank Thee for Thy heart's desire
As all Thy travail we review.

5   We eat the bread and drink the wine,
And to Thy sweetness we are led;
In spirit each receiving Thee,
Our spirits with Thyself are fed.

6   We long to eat and drink e'en more,
To take Thyself in spirit thus,
Till Thou shalt all our being fill
And true remembrance have from us.

*Composition for prophecy with main point and
sub-points:* _____

_____

_____

_____

_____

_____

_____

_____

_____

_____

_____

_____

_____

_____

_____

_____

_____

_____

_____

_____

_____

_____

_____

_____

_____

_____

_____

_____

_____

_____

The All-inclusive Christ
in the Gospel of Matthew

Scripture Reading: Matt. 1:1; 16:16; 4:16; 9:12, 15-17, 36, 38; 15:26-27; 28:18-19

Day 1

I. Christ is the son of David and the son of Abraham (Matt. 1:1):
  A. Solomon, the son of David, is a type of Christ inheriting the kingdom (2 Sam. 7:12b, 13b; Jer. 23:5; Luke 1:32-33), having wisdom and speaking the word of wisdom (Matt. 12:42), and building the temple of God (2 Sam. 7:13a).
  B. Isaac, the son of Abraham, is a type of Christ as the promised One who brought the blessing to all the nations (Gen. 22:18; Gal. 3:16, 14), who was offered to God unto death and was resurrected (Gen. 22:1-12; Heb. 11:17, 19), and who will receive the bride (Gen. 24:67; John 3:29; Rev. 19:7).

II. Christ is the heavenly King (Matt. 2:1-2; 21:5):
  A. Matthew proves that Jesus is the King, the Messiah prophesied in the Old Testament (1:1, 17; 2:1-2; 27:11, 37).
  B. The heavenly King did not come with haughty splendor but with gentle, humble meekness (21:5).

III. The Lord Jesus is the Christ, the Son of the living God (16:16):
  A. *The Christ* refers to the anointed One of God and speaks of the Lord's commission to accomplish God's eternal purpose through His crucifixion, resurrection, ascension, and second coming (vv. 21, 27).
  B. *The Son of the living God* speaks of His person, which embodies the Father and consummates in the Spirit for a full expression of the Triune God (John 14:10-11a; 1 Cor. 15:45b).

Day 2

IV. Christ is the Son of Man (Matt. 8:20; 11:19; 13:37; 16:13):

   A. Christ is the man who brings God's dominion to earth and makes God's name excellent on earth (9:6; 12:8; 13:41; 16:27-28).

   B. In order for the kingdom of the heavens to be established, the Lord Jesus stood as a victorious man— a man who could defeat Satan and withstand any hardship, opposition, or attack (4:4; 12:40; 26:64).

V. Christ is the Baptizer (3:11):

   A. The Lord's baptism in the Holy Spirit, which is based on His redemption, initiated the kingdom of the heavens, bringing His believers into the kingdom of the heavens (v. 12a).

   B. The Lord's baptism in fire, which is based on His judgment, will conclude the kingdom of the heavens, putting the unbelievers into the lake of fire (v. 12b).

VI. Christ is the light of life shining in the darkness of death (4:12-16):

   A. Christ's ministry for the kingdom of the heavens began not with earthly power but with heavenly light.

   B. The Lord Jesus attracted the disciples to Himself as the great light for the establishment of the kingdom of the heavens.

Day 3 **VII. Christ is the Physician and the Bridegroom (9:9-15):**

   A. He came as a Physician to heal and enliven us so that we might be reconstituted to be citizens of the kingdom of the heavens (vv. 9-13).

   B. We need to appreciate Him as the Bridegroom that we might have the enjoyment of living in His presence (vv. 14-15).

VIII. Christ is the unfulled cloth for making a new garment (v. 16; Luke 5:36):

   A. From His incarnation to His crucifixion, He was the unfulled cloth for making a new garment.

   B. Through His death and resurrection, Christ was made a new garment to cover us as our righteousness before God that we might be justified by God and be acceptable to Him (15:22; Gal. 3:27; 1 Cor. 1:30).

IX. **The individual Christ is the new wine, and the corporate Christ is the fresh wineskin (Matt. 9:17):**
   A. The new wine signifies Christ as the new life, full of vigor and cheering strength, stirring us to excitement and satisfying us.
   B. The fresh wineskin signifies the corporate Christ, the outward container that holds the new wine (1 Cor. 12:12).

X. **Christ is the Shepherd (Matt. 9:36):**
   A. In verse 36 *harassed* refers to the sheep's being skinned by cruel shepherds and thus suffering pain, and *cast away* refers to the sheep's being abandoned by wicked shepherds and falling into a distressed condition in which they are homeless and helpless.
   B. In His ministry for the establishing of His heavenly kingdom, the Lord Jesus ministered as a Shepherd (v. 36).

Day 4 XI. **Christ is the Lord of the harvest (vv. 37-38):**

Korean
   A. As the Lord of the harvest, the Lord who owns the crop, Christ establishes His kingdom with things of life that can grow and multiply (v. 38).
   B. If we see the vision of Christ as the Lord of the harvest, we will beseech Him to thrust out workers into His harvest (vv. 37-38).

the crops become the workers through prayer

XII. **Christ is the Friend of sinners and the wisdom of God (11:19):**
   A. As the Friend of sinners, Christ sympathizes with their problems and senses their grief (v. 19a).
   B. Whatever Christ did was done by the wisdom of God, which is Himself; this wisdom was vindicated by His wise works (v. 19b; 1 Cor. 1:24, 30).

XIII. **Christ is the One who gives rest (Matt. 11:28-30):**
   A. To take the Lord's yoke is to take the will of the Father and to be constrained by the will of the Father (v. 29; John 4:34; 5:30; 6:38).

B. Because the Lord was always satisfied with the Father's will, He always had rest in His heart; now He asks us to learn from Him (Matt. 11:28-30).

Day 5 **XIV. Christ as the Son of Man is Lord of the Sabbath (12:8):**

A. As the Lord of the Sabbath, He had the right to change the regulations concerning the Sabbath.

B. He was above all rituals and regulations; He could do whatever He liked on the Sabbath, and whatever He did was justified by Himself.

XV. Christ is greater than the temple (v. 6):

A. In verse 6 we have a type-fulfilling turn from the temple to a person who is greater than the temple.

B. Since the priests were guiltless in acting on the Sabbath in the temple, the Lord's disciples were guiltless in acting on the Sabbath in Christ, who is greater than the temple.

XVI. Christ is the greater Jonah (vv. 39-41; 16:4):

A. Jonah is a type of Christ in His death, burial, and resurrection (12:39-41).

B. For the evil and adulterous Jewish and religious generation, the Lord Jesus would do nothing but die and be resurrected as the greatest sign to them that they might be saved if they would believe (16:4).

XVII. Christ is the greater Solomon (12:42):

A. Solomon is a type of Christ, the King, who is building the church, making it the temple of God (1 Kings 6:2; 1 Cor. 3:16-17; Eph. 2:21).

B. According to spiritual significance, Christ as the greater Jonah precedes Christ as the greater Solomon, for first He had to die and be resurrected and then build the church as the temple of God (Matt. 16:18, 21).

Day 6 **XVIII. Christ is the One who found a treasure hidden in the field, and He is the merchant seeking fine pearls (13:44-46):**

A. Christ found the kingdom of the heavens, and in His joy He went to the cross to sell all that He had to buy the field, that is, redeem the created and lost earth, for the kingdom (v. 44).

B. Christ was seeking the church for His kingdom, and He went to the cross and sold all that He had and bought it for the kingdom (vv. 45-46).

XIX. **Christ is the bread and the crumbs under the table (15:21-38):**
A. God's economy is not a matter of outward things but of Christ coming into us as food (vv. 26, 34, 36).
B. We need to take in the edible Christ by eating Him as bread, even as the crumbs under the table (v. 27).

XX. **Christ in His humanity is the resurrected One with all authority in heaven and on earth (28:18-19):**
A. In His humanity, as the Son of Man and the heavenly King, all authority was given to Christ after His resurrection (v. 18).
B. Because the Gospel of Matthew is concerned for the kingdom and the kingdom requires authority, in Matthew Christ's resurrection is a matter of authority for discipling the nations (v. 19).

Morning Nourishment

Matt. The book of the generation of Jesus Christ, the son of
1:1   David, the son of Abraham.
Matt. ...Magi from the east arrived in Jerusalem, saying,
2:1-2 Where is He who has been born King of the Jews?...
16:16 And Simon Peter answered and said, You are the
       Christ, the Son of the living God.

Christ is the son of David (Matt. 22:42, 45; Rev. 22:16). Solomon, the son of David, was a type of Christ in three main aspects. First, he was a type of Christ inheriting the kingdom (2 Sam. 7:12b, 13; Jer. 23:5; Luke 1:32-33). Second, Solomon had wisdom and spoke the word of wisdom. In Matthew 12...Christ referred to Himself as the greater Solomon (v. 42). A greater than Solomon was there, and He spoke words of wisdom. No human words are as wise as the words of Christ. Third, Solomon built the temple of God (2 Sam. 7:13). As the son of David, Christ builds up God's temple, the church. (*Life-study of Matthew*, p. 9)

Today's Reading

Christ is also the son of Abraham. This book of generation says only that Christ is the son of David and the son of Abraham, not the son of anyone else. In the Old Testament there was a clear prophecy that Christ would be the son of Abraham. Isaac was a type of Christ. With Isaac as a type of Christ there were also three main aspects. First, Isaac brought the blessing to all nations, both Jews and Gentiles (Gen. 22:18a; Gal. 3:16, 14). Second, he was offered to God unto death and was resurrected (Gen. 22:1-12; Heb. 11:17, 19). Third, he received the bride (Gen. 24:67). This is a type of Christ as the promised One who brought the blessing to all nations, who was also offered to death, who was resurrected, and who, after His resurrection, will receive His bride (John 3:29; Rev. 19:7). One day the Holy Spirit, typified by Abraham's servant, will bring the spiritual, divine, heavenly Rebekah to her heavenly Isaac.

The son of Abraham received the bride, and the son of David built up the temple. With Christ, the bride is the temple, and the temple is the bride. This is why it says that Christ is the son of

Abraham and the son of David. He offered Himself unto death and was resurrected, now He is building God's temple, and in the future He will receive the bride. Christ also spoke wisdom and brought God's blessing to all nations. He is the One to fulfill all of these things. In the four Gospels we can find each of these six aspects.

Matthew uses the phrase, "Who is called Christ" (Matt. 1:16). In Luke's genealogy, the title Christ is not mentioned. Luke mentions the name Jesus because Luke proves that the Lord came to be a man, not to be the anointed One, the King, the Messiah. Matthew, on the contrary, proves that Jesus is the King, the Messiah prophesied in the Old Testament. Hence, he added the word, "Who is called Christ."

The significance of the Lord's riding on a donkey [21:4-5] is not smallness, but meekness. The heavenly King came not with haughty splendor, but with gentle, humble meekness. This impression of meekness is strengthened by the colt accompanying a donkey to bear the meek King. The Lord Jesus did not ride into Jerusalem proudly on a horse. He came mounted upon a little donkey, even a small colt. No earthly king would do this. The Lord Jesus seemed to be telling His disciples, "Take the donkey and the little colt. I shall ride upon the beast of burden, but the colt must go along too in order to show My meekness. This will help the people see how meek the heavenly King is."

After the Lord asked His disciples to say who they thought He was, Simon Peter answered and said, "You are the Christ, the Son of the living God" (16:16). The Christ, as the anointed One of God, refers to the Lord's commission; whereas the Son of the living God, as the second of the Triune God, refers to His person. His commission is to accomplish God's eternal purpose through His crucifixion, resurrection, ascension, and second advent, whereas His person embodies the Father and issues in the Spirit for a full expression of the Triune God. (*Life-study of Matthew,* pp. 9-10, 47, 661-662, 565-566)

Further Reading: Life-study of Matthew, msgs. 1, 4, 47, 56

Enlightenment and inspiration: _____

_____

_____

_____

Morning Nourishment

Matt. I baptize you in water unto repentance, but He who is
3:11 coming after me is stronger than I, whose sandals I
am not worthy to carry. He Himself will baptize you
in the Holy Spirit and fire.

4:16 "The people sitting in darkness have seen a great
light; and to those sitting in the region and shadow of
death, to them light has risen."

Chapter one of Genesis says that God created the earth and
that He created man in His own image with the intention that
man would exercise His dominion over the animals, the fowl,
and the fish. This is the kingdom on earth. However, man failed.
But Psalm 8 follows with a prophecy. Verse 1 of this Psalm says,
"O Jehovah our Lord, / How excellent is Your name / In all the
earth." When the earth is God's dominion, His name will be sanctified and made excellent on the earth. Speaking of man, Psalm
8:6 says, "You have caused Him to rule over the works of Your
hands; / You have put all things under His feet." The following
verses reveal that man has dominion over the beasts of the field,
the fowl of the air, and the fish of the sea. Hebrews 2 reveals that
the man described in Psalm 8 firstly is Christ. Christ is the man
who brings in God's dominion to earth and makes God's name
excellent on earth. (*Life-study of Matthew*, pp. 476-477)

Today's Reading

For the kingdom of the heavens to be established, there was the
need of a man like Jesus. Throughout Matthew 26, the Lord Jesus
stood in the position of a man, not in the position of the Son of God.
In order for the kingdom of the heavens to be established, He
stood as a man, a successful man, a victorious man, as a man that
could withstand any hardship, defeat, opposition, and attack.

Matthew 3:11 says, "I baptize you in water unto repentance,
but He who is coming after me is stronger than I, whose sandals I
am not worthy to carry. He Himself will baptize you in the Holy
Spirit and fire." In this verse John seemed to be saying, "I have
come to baptize you with water, to terminate you, to bury you. But

the One who comes after me is mightier than I. He will baptize you with the Spirit and fire. Whether He will baptize you with the Spirit or with fire depends on whether or not you repent. If you repent, He will put you into the Spirit. But if you continue to be a brood of vipers, He will certainly baptize you in the lake of fire. This means that He will put you into the fire of hell."

John's baptism was only for repentance, to usher people to faith in the Lord. The Lord's baptism is either for eternal life in the Holy Spirit or for eternal perdition in fire. The Lord's baptism in the Holy Spirit began the kingdom of the heavens, bringing His believers into the kingdom of the heavens, whereas His baptism in fire will terminate the kingdom of the heavens, putting the unbelievers into the lake of fire. Hence, the Lord's baptism in the Holy Spirit, based upon His redemption, is the beginning of the kingdom of the heavens, whereas His baptism in fire, based upon His judgment, is its ending.

The new King's ministry for the kingdom of the heavens began not with earthly power, but with heavenly light, which was the King Himself as the light of life, shining in the shadow of death. When the Lord began His ministry as light, He made no display of power and authority. He walked upon the seashore as a common person. But as He came to those four disciples by the Sea of Galilee, He shined upon them like a great light, shining in the darkness and in the region of the shadow of death. At that juncture, Peter, Andrew, James, and John were enlightened and attracted. We have pointed out that John the Baptist was a great magnet. But the Lord Jesus is the greatest magnet of all. As He shined upon those four disciples, they were attracted and captured. They immediately forsook their jobs and followed this little Nazarene.

Moreover, when the Lord Jesus called these four disciples, He did not start a movement or a revolution. Rather, He attracted the disciples to Himself for the establishment of the kingdom of the heavens. (*Life-study of Matthew*, pp. 794, 113-114, 156-157)

Further Reading: Life-study of Matthew, msgs. 9, 12

Enlightenment and inspiration: _____

_____

_____

_____

Morning Nourishment

Matt. And Jesus said to them, The sons of the bridechamber
9:15 cannot mourn as long as the bridegroom is with them,
can they? But days will come when the bridegroom
will be taken away from them, and then they will fast.
17 Neither do they put new wine into old wineskins;
otherwise, the wineskins burst, and the wine pours
out, and the wineskins are ruined; but they put new
wine into fresh wineskins, and both are preserved.

The Lord took the opportunity given Him by the Pharisees'
question to give a very sweet revelation of Himself as the Physician. In Matthew 9:12 we see the Lord's reply to the Pharisees'
question: "Those who are strong have no need of a physician, but
those who are ill." The Lord was telling the Pharisees that these
tax collectors and sinners were patients, sick ones, and that to
them the Lord was not a judge, but a physician, a healer....He
came to minister as a physician, to heal, recover, enliven, and save
them, so that they might be reconstituted to be His new and heavenly citizens, with whom He could establish His heavenly kingdom on this corrupted earth. (Life-study of Matthew, pp. 329-330)

Today's Reading

The kingly Savior firstly healed His followers, then made
them the sons of the bridechamber [Matt. 9:14-15]. Eventually
He will make them His bride. They should appropriate Him not
only as their Physician for the recovery of their life, but also as
their Bridegroom for a living of enjoyment in His presence. They
were at a joyful wedding with Him, not at a sorrowful funeral
without Him.

[Matthew 9:16 says, "No one puts a patch of unfulled cloth on
an old garment, for that which fills it up pulls away from the garment, and a worse tear is made."] The Lord Jesus likened Himself to a piece of unfulled cloth. This points to what He was
between His incarnation and His crucifixion. During this period
of time He was unfulled cloth, new cloth that had never been
fulled or dealt with. Through His death and resurrection this new

cloth was dealt with and was made a new garment. The Lord's intention was to give Himself to us not as a piece of unfulled cloth, but as a complete, finished garment that we might put on as our righteousness to be justified before God. After His death and resurrection, He was made the finished garment for us to put on so that we may attend His wedding. Thus, He is not only the Bridegroom, but also our wedding garment that qualifies us to attend His wedding feast.

The individual Christ is the new wine, the exciting life inwardly, and the corporate Christ is the fresh wineskin, the container to hold the new wine outwardly. With the kingdom people, it is not a matter of fasting or of any other religious practice, but a matter of the church life with Christ as their content. Christ came not to establish an earthly religion of rituals, but a heavenly kingdom of life, not with any dead religious practices, but with Himself, the living person, as the Physician, the Bridegroom, the unfulled cloth, and the new wine to His followers as their full enjoyment that they might be the fresh wineskin to contain Him and become the constituents of His kingdom.

Matthew 9:36 says, "And seeing the crowds, He was moved with compassion for them, because they were harassed and cast away like sheep not having a shepherd." This indicates that the heavenly King considered the Israelites as sheep and Himself as the Shepherd. When Christ came to the Jews the first time, they were like lepers, paralytics, demon-possessed, and all manner of pitiful persons, because they had no shepherd to care for them. Now in His kingly ministry for the establishing of His heavenly kingdom, He ministered to them not only as a Physician, but also as a Shepherd, as prophesied in Isaiah 53:6 and 40:11.

In the midst of the situation portrayed in verse 36 the Lord revealed Himself as the Shepherd. This is a further revelation. He is not only the Physician and the Bridegroom, but also the Shepherd. (*Life-study of Matthew*, pp. 335-336, 338-339, 344, 358)

Further Reading: Life-study of Matthew, msgs. 27-28

Enlightenment and inspiration: _____

_____

_____

_____

Morning Nourishment

Matt. **Therefore beseech the Lord of the harvest that He**
9:38 **would thrust out workers into His harvest.**
11:29-30 **Take My yoke upon you and learn from Me, for I am**
meek and lowly in heart, and you will find rest for
your souls. For My yoke is easy and My burden is light.

The King of the heavenly kingdom considered Himself not
only the Shepherd of the sheep, but also the Lord of the harvest.
His kingdom is established with things of life that can grow and
multiply. He is the Lord who owns this crop. We are both the flock
and the crop.

We all need to see a vision of the Lord Jesus as the Lord of the
harvest. In Matthew 9:38 the Lord told us to beseech the Lord of
the harvest that He may thrust out workers into His harvest.
Firstly, in His economy, God has a plan to accomplish. Then His
economy requires His people to beseech, to pray, for it. In answering
their prayer, He will accomplish what they have prayed concerning
His plan. Many times when we sense the need for workers, we
sound out the call for help. But from now on, whenever you sense
the need for workers, you must firstly pray to the Lord of the harvest....Praying...will make a difference. To pray...means that we
have seen a vision that our Christ, the kingly One, the Shepherd, is
the Lord of the harvest. (*Life-study of Matthew*, pp. 359-360)

Today's Reading

Whenever you pray that the Lord would send reapers into His
harvest, you honor Him very much. How different this is from
inviting people to help you in your work! When you do that, you do
not honor Christ as the Lord of the harvest. Rather, it is a matter
of your work, not of His harvest. You become the master of that
work, and He is not considered as the Lord of the harvest. Therefore, we need to call on Him and say, "Lord, You are the Lord of the
harvest. The work in this field is Yours, and this harvest is Your
crop. We call on You for Your crop. Lord, send Your reapers."

Christ is not only the Savior, but also the friend of sinners,
sympathizing with their problems and sensing their griefs.

In Matthew 11:19 the Lord said, "Yet wisdom is justified by her works." Wisdom is Christ (1 Cor. 1:24, 30). Whatever Christ did was done by the wisdom of God, which is Himself. This wisdom was justified, vindicated, by His wise works, His wise deeds. In this verse some authorities read "children" instead of "works." The kingdom people are the children of wisdom, who justify Christ and His deeds and follow Him as their wisdom. Christ is justified by the kingdom people, who know when to eat and when not to eat and who recognize the playing of the flute and the singing of the dirge, knowing when to rejoice and when to repent.

In Matthew 11:29 and 30 we have the way to rest....The Lord's yoke is to take the will of the Father. It is not to be regulated or controlled by any obligations of the law or religion, nor to be enslaved by any work, but to be constrained by the will of the Father. The Lord lived such a life, caring for nothing but the will of His Father (John 4:34; 5:30; 6:38). He submitted Himself fully to the Father's will (Matt. 26:39, 42)....In the Lord's recovery we all have been yoked. How good it is to be yoked! The Lord's yoke is easy and His burden is light. The Lord's yoke is the Father's will, and His burden is the work to carry out the Father's will.

In all the opposition the Lord was meek, and in all the rejection He was lowly in heart. He submitted Himself fully to the will of His Father, not wanting to do anything for Himself nor expecting to gain something for Himself. Hence, regardless of the situation, He had rest in His heart. He was fully satisfied with His Father's will.

The Lord said that if we take His yoke upon us and learn from Him, we shall find rest for our souls. The rest we find by taking the Lord's yoke and learning from Him is for our souls. It is an inward rest....Christ, the heavenly King, always submitted to the Father's will, taking God's will as His portion and not resisting anything. Hence, He was always at rest. (*Life-study of Matthew*, pp. 360, 385, 391-392)

Further Reading: Life-study of Matthew, msgs. 29, 31; *The God-man Living*, msgs. 12-13

Enlightenment and inspiration: _____

_____

_____

_____

Morning Nourishment

Matt. **But I say to you that something greater than the**
12:6 **temple is here.**
8 **For the Son of Man is Lord of the Sabbath.**
41-42 **...Behold, something more than Jonah is here...**
Behold, something more than Solomon is here.

In Matthew 12:8 the Lord said, "For the Son of Man is Lord of the Sabbath." How bold the Lord Jesus was! He won the case, and the Pharisees, who were shocked and frightened, were silenced. They had nothing to say. The Lord's telling the Pharisees that He was Lord of the Sabbath was like someone today telling a high-way patrolman that he is lord of the highway.

In verse 8 the Lord indicated a third change, a right-asserting change from the Sabbath to the Lord of the Sabbath. As the Lord of the Sabbath, He had the right to change the regulations concerning the Sabbath. Thus, the Lord gave the condemning Pharisees a threefold verdict. He was the real David, the greater temple, and the Lord of the Sabbath. Therefore, He could do whatever He liked on the Sabbath, and whatever He did was justified by Himself. He was above all rituals and regulations. Because He was there, no attention should be paid to any rituals and regulations. (*Life-study of Matthew*, pp. 399-400)

Today's Reading

In Matthew 12:6 the Lord declared, "But I say to you that something greater than the temple is here." What boldness the Lord had! He was a Nazarene, but as He stood before the Phari-sees He seemed to be saying, "Look at Me. I am greater than the temple." The Pharisees must have been shocked to such an extent that they could not say anything.

The Lord's revealing to the Pharisees that He was greater than the temple was another change, a type-fulfilling change from the temple to a person. In the case of David [1 Sam. 21:1-6], it was a change from one age to another. In this case, a case concern-ing the priests, it was a change from the temple to a person who is greater than the temple. Since the priests were guiltless in doing things on the Sabbath in the temple, how could the Lord's disciples be guilty in doing things on the Sabbath in Him who is greater than the temple? In the first case, it was the king breaking the Levitical regulation; in the second case, it was the priests breaking the sabbatical regulation. In the Scriptures, neither was guilty. Hence, what the Lord did here was scripturally right.... This was a change from the type to the reality.

Matthew 16:4 says, "An evil and adulterous generation seeks after a sign, and a sign shall not be given to it, except the sign of Jonah. And He left them and went away." Jonah was the prophet who turned from Israel to the Gentiles and was put into the belly of the great fish. After remaining there for three days, he emerged to become a sign to that generation for repentance (Jonah 1:2, 17; 2:2-10). This was a type of Christ, the prophet sent by God to His people (Deut. 18:15, 18), who would turn from Israel to the Gentiles, and who would be buried in the heart of the earth for three days and then be resurrected, becoming a sign to this generation for salvation. The Lord's word here implies that to that evil and adulterous, Jewish and religious generation, the Lord would do nothing but die and be resurrected as a sign, the greatest sign to them, that they might be saved if they would believe.

In the Lord's conversation with the Pharisees, suddenly another sign appeared: the sign of Solomon. Matthew 12:42 says, "The queen of the south will rise up in the judgment with this generation and will condemn it, because she came from the ends of the earth to hear the wisdom of Solomon, and behold, something more than Solomon is here." Christ, as the Son of David to be the King, is greater than Solomon the king. Solomon built the temple of God and spoke the word of wisdom, and to him the Gentile queen came (1 Kings 6:2; 10:1-8). This also is a type of Christ, who is building the church to be the temple of God and speaking the word of wisdom, and to Him the Gentile seekers turn. (*Life-study of Matthew*, pp. 398-399, 560, 419)

Further Reading: Life-study of Matthew, msgs. 32, 34

Enlightenment and inspiration: _____

Christ's death solve all problems between God & man.

Morning Nourishment

Matt. **The kingdom of the heavens is like a treasure hid-**
13:44-46 **den in the field, which a man found and hid, and in**
his joy goes and sells all that he has, and buys that
field. Again, the kingdom of the heavens is like a
merchant seeking fine pearls; and finding one pearl
of great value, he went and sold all that he had and
bought it.

Matthew 13:44 says that the kingdom of the heavens is like a
treasure hidden in the field "which a man found and hid, and in
his joy goes and sells all that he has, and buys that field." The
man here is Christ, who found the kingdom of the heavens in
4:12 to 12:23, hid it in 12:24 to 13:43, and in His joy went to the
cross in 16:21; 17:22-23; 20:18-19; and 26:1 to 27:52 to sell all He
had and buy that field—to redeem the created and lost earth—
for the kingdom. Christ first found the treasure when He came
out to minister, declaring, "Repent, for the kingdom of the heavens has drawn near" [4:17]. When the Jews' rejection of the Lord
reached its peak, He forsook them. From that time onward, He
hid the treasure. Then He went to the cross to buy not only the
treasure, but also the field, and He thereby redeemed the earth
created by God.

Christ went to the cross to redeem the God-created earth
because within the earth there was the kingdom, the treasure.
For the kingdom, for this treasure, Christ redeemed the earth
created by God. (*Life-study of Matthew,* pp. 477-478)

Today's Reading

Matthew 13:45 and 46 say, "Again, the kingdom of the heavens is like a merchant seeking fine pearls; and finding one pearl
of great value, he went and sold all that he had and bought it."
The merchant in verse 45 is also Christ, who was seeking the
church for His kingdom. After finding it in 16:18 and 18:17,
He went to the cross and sold all He had and bought it for the
kingdom.

In today's religion people are following outward practices.

But God's economy is not a matter of outward things; it is a matter of Christ coming into us inwardly. For this, we need to take Christ in by eating Him.

Before you came into the church, you never heard a word about eating Jesus, for all the teachings in religion are concerned with the outward washing of hands, not with presenting the edible Jesus to people. But this ministry has come here with the commission to minister the edible Jesus to His believers....We need to take Jesus in. Hallelujah, today Jesus is not on the table! He is under the table [Matt. 15:21-28 and footnotes]. He has been cast off the table by the Israelites, and now He is in the Gentile world. All of us, including me, are dirty, pagan dogs. Nevertheless, we can praise the Lord that we are dogs, because the very bread of life from the heavens is now where the dogs are. If the bread were on the table, it would not be available to us. But today the bread is under the table where the dogs are. We need the edible Christ who is now so near to us.

Matthew 28:18 says, "And Jesus came and spoke to them, saying, All authority has been given to Me in heaven and on earth." In His divinity as the only begotten Son of God, the Lord had authority over all. However, in His humanity as the Son of Man to be the King of the heavenly kingdom, all authority in heaven and on earth was given to Him after His resurrection.

Matthew's concern was for the kingdom, and the kingdom requires authority. The Gospel of John reveals that we need life to care for the little lambs and to feed the Lord's flock. But in Matthew 28 there is no word about feeding the lambs. In Matthew the Lord commands the disciples to disciple all the nations (v. 19) to make all the nations part of the kingdom. This requires authority. Therefore, in John resurrection is a matter of life, power, breath, and shepherding. However, in Matthew it is a matter of righteousness, authority, and discipling the nations. (*Life-study of Matthew,* pp. 478, 551-552, 826-827)

Further Reading: Life-study of Matthew, msgs. 39, 46, 72

Enlightenment and inspiration: _____

_____

_____

_____

Hymns, #190

1 O Lord, as we consider Thee,
   We worship Thee for all Thou art;
   Thou art so rich, so wonderful,
   So dear and precious to our heart.

      What Thou art meets our every need!
      Our hearts o'erflow with praise to Thee!
      All our desires Thou dost exceed
      And satisfy continually.

2 Thou art the very God in truth,
   The God who is both love and light;
   The God who is to us our life,
   The God in whom we all delight.

3 Thou also art a man indeed,
   A man so fine, so good, so pure;
   A man in whom our God delights,
   A man who can our love secure.

4 Thou even art a lowly slave,
   A slave of God to serve for us;
   Obedient to the cross's death
   That we might be delivered thus.

5 Thou art, beside all these, a King,
   A King in life and love to reign,
   By God anointed with His pow'r
   To rule with us in His domain.

6 Dear Lord, as we remember Thee,
   We thus partake of all Thou art;
   As we enjoy Thyself in love,
   We share Thee as Thy counterpart.

Composition for prophecy with main point and sub-points: _____

_____

_____

_____

_____

_____

_____

_____

_____

_____

_____

_____

_____

_____

_____

_____

_____

_____

_____

_____

_____

_____

_____

_____

_____

_____

_____

_____

_____

_____

_____

_____

_____

_____

_____

Experiencing the Indwelling Christ

Scripture Reading: John 14:16-18, 20; Rom. 8:9-10; Gal.
2:20a; 4:19; Eph. 3:17a

Day 1

I. **Christ is a mystery, and His indwelling is also
a mystery (Col. 1:27):**
   A. Christ's indwelling is very real and intimate because it takes place within us and is intimately
   related to us (John 14:20; Eph. 3:17a).
   B. The experience of the indwelling Christ is a real
   and subjective matter (Rom. 8:10; 2 Cor. 13:5; Gal.
   4:19).

II. **While the Lord Jesus was on earth, He was the
Comforter outside His disciples, but after His
resurrection He became the Comforter inside
His disciples (John 14:16-18, 20):**
   A. The Greek word for *Comforter* means "advocate,"
   "one alongside who takes care of our cause, our
   affairs."
   B. While the Lord Jesus was on earth, He was with
   His disciples in an outward way as a tender, caring Comforter; although His physical presence
   with the disciples was wonderful, He could be with
   them only in an outward way since He was still in
   the flesh, limited by space and time (v. 16).
   C. In order to be the indwelling Comforter, the Comforter inside the disciples, it was necessary for the
   Lord Jesus to pass through death and enter into
   resurrection to become the Spirit of reality, the
   life-giving Spirit (v. 17; 1 Cor. 15:45b):

Day 2

   1. The most precious result of our faith in Christ
   is that we receive Christ into us; He is now
   able to enter into us to be with us at any time
   and in any place as the Comforter within us
   (John 1:12-13; 3:15; 14:16-17).
   2. The "He" who is the Spirit of reality in verse 17
   becomes the "I" who is the Lord Himself in
   verse 18; this means that the Christ who was

in the flesh went through death and resurrection to become the life-giving Spirit, the pneumatic Christ (1 Cor. 15:45b; 2 Cor. 3:17a).

D. The Gospel of John reveals that Christ became flesh to be the Lamb of God and that in resurrection He became the life-giving Spirit, another Comforter, to breathe Himself into the disciples (1:14, 29; 14:16-17; 20:22):

1. It is as the Spirit that He was breathed into His disciples and that He can live in them and they can live because of Him (14:19-20).

2. The Holy Spirit in 20:22 is actually the resurrected Christ Himself, because this Spirit is His breath; the Spirit is the breath of the resurrected Christ.

Day 3

III. **As the subject of Romans, the gospel of God concerns Christ as the Spirit living within the believers after His resurrection (1:1, 3-4):**

A. Christ has resurrected and has become the life-giving Spirit; He is no longer merely the Christ outside the believers but the Christ within them (8:9-10).

B. The gospel in the Epistle to the Romans is the gospel of the One who is now indwelling His believers as their subjective Savior (1:1, 3-4; 8:10; 5:10).

IV. **The apostle Paul is a pattern of a believer who experienced the indwelling Christ (1 Tim. 1:16):**

A. "It pleased God...to reveal His Son in me" (Gal. 1:15a, 16a):

1. To reveal the Son of God brings pleasure to God; nothing is more pleasing to God than the unveiling of the living person of the Son of God.

2. We need to be brought into a state where we are full of the revelation of the Son of God and thereby become a new creation with Christ living in us.

Day 4

B. "I am crucified with Christ; and it is no longer I who live, but it is Christ who lives in me" (2:20a):

1. Paul did not say that the (life) of Christ lived in him but that Christ, the (person,) lived in him.

Mike

2. God's economy is that the "I" be crucified in Christ's death and that Christ live in us in His resurrection.

Ben

C. "My children, with whom I travail again in birth until Christ is formed in you" (4:19):

Paul

  1. To have Christ formed in us is to have Christ grown in us in full.

Crip

  2. Christ has been born into us, He is now living in us in our Christian life, and He will be formed in us at our maturity.

Grace

D. "As many of you as were baptized into Christ have put on Christ" (3:27):

Larry

  1. To be baptized is to be immersed into the reality of the person of Christ.

Kathy

  2. We have put on the pneumatic Christ as our clothing; this means that, as our person, Christ is not only our inner being but also our outward expression.

Tony

Day 5

Korean

E. "That Christ may make His home in your hearts through faith" (Eph. 3:17a):

  1. God the Father is exercising His authority through God the Spirit to strengthen us into the inner man that God the Son may make His home deep downward in our hearts.

  2. If we allow Christ to have all the room within us and if we give Him the full right and full liberty to do whatever He wants within us, then our heart will become His home.

F. "God is my witness how I long after you all in the inward parts of Christ Jesus" (Phil. 1:8):

  1. Paul did not live in his natural inner being; he lived a life in the inward parts of Christ, experienced Christ in His inward parts, and was one with Christ in His inward parts.

  2. Paul did not keep his own inward parts but took Christ's inward parts as his; Paul's inner

being was reconstituted with the inward parts of Christ.

Day 6

G. "Let this mind be in you, which was also in Christ Jesus" (2:5):

  1. To let Christ's mind be in us is to allow the indwelling Christ to live in us by denying our natural mind and taking His mind.

  2. If we want to experience the indwelling Christ and live Him, we need to deny our mind and have our mind replaced by the mind of Christ (1:21a).

H. "For also what I have forgiven, if I have forgiven anything, it is for your sake in the person of Christ" (2 Cor. 2:10b):

  1. Paul lived Christ in the closest and most intimate contact with Him, acting according to the index of His eyes.

  2. Paul was a person who was one with Christ, full of Christ, and saturated with Christ; he truly experienced the indwelling Christ (Col. 3:11).

manifested to His saints

Morning Nourishment

Col. 1:27 To whom God willed to make known what are the riches of the glory of this mystery among the Gentiles, which is Christ in you, the hope of glory.

Rom. 8:10 But if Christ is in you, though the body is dead because of sin, the spirit is life because of righteousness.

Through my many years of studying the Word, I can tell you that the most crucial items in the New Testament are the indwelling Christ and Christ's indwelling. The New Testament not only speaks about a mysterious person, Christ, but it also speaks about one thing concerning this mysterious person, that is, that Christ indwells His believers.

We know that Christ is truly a mystery, and His indwelling is even more a mystery. Even so, Christ's indwelling is very real and intimate because it is not something that takes place outside of us but rather something that transpires within us and is intimately related to us. Therefore, this is a very real and subjective matter. (*The Subjective Experience of the Indwelling Christ,* pp. 46, 43)

Today's Reading

In John 14:16 the Lord Jesus said, "I will ask the Father, and He will give you another Comforter." The Greek word for *Comforter* is difficult to translate because it is a very particular word; its anglicized form is *paraclete.* The word refers to one who is called to your side to wait on you, to take care of you, and to bear all your responsibilities. If you are sick, he is both the doctor and the nurse to take care of you. If you have a legal case, he is the lawyer to help you handle the case and go to court to represent you in the lawsuit. Moreover, if you encounter any problem in your daily life, he is your counselor. He can solve your problem, and you can pour out your heart to him and enjoy his kind protection. This Greek word implies a great deal. First John 2:1 says, "We have an Advocate with the Father, Jesus Christ the Righteous." This Advocate is our Comforter. The Greek word for *Advocate* is the same as that for *Comforter;* the two titles refer to the same One.

Originally, the Lord Jesus was God over all and the Creator of

the universe (Rom. 9:5; John 1:3). One day He humbled Himself
to become a man by being conceived and born of a virgin in a man-
ger. He lived in the despised city of Nazareth and grew up in a
poor carpenter's home. When He was thirty years old, He went
out to preach the word, heal the sick, cast out demons, perform
signs and wonders, and teach the truth. He was with His disciples
for three and a half years and was very thoughtful of them. He
knew their problems and was able to meet all their needs. Par-
ents love their children, yet often they are unable to render any
help to their children when their children have problems. The
Lord Jesus, however, was not only kind and thoughtful but also
omniscient and omnipotent. He lived, walked, ate, and drank
with His disciples. He solved all their problems and ministered to
all their needs. He was not only their Doctor and Nurse but also
their Lawyer and Counselor. He was truly their Comforter.

While the Lord Jesus was on the earth, He was with His disciples in an outward way for three and a half years; He was a tender,
caring Comforter. However, after three and a half years, suddenly
one day He told His disciples that He was going away from them
and was going to Him who sent Him (John 16:5). The disciples
were shocked by His word and felt sorrowful. Nevertheless, He told
them not to be sorrowful, saying, "It is expedient for you that I go
away" (v. 7). This was because, while at that time His physical presence with the disciples was wonderful, He could be among them
only in an outward way since He was still in the flesh, limited by
time and space. He could not be with His disciples if they were at
the Sea of Galilee in the north while He was in the temple in Jerusalem to the south. Therefore, He had to go and have a change to
become the life-giving Spirit. Thus, He would be able to enter into
them to be with them at any time and in any place as the Comforter within them. For the disciples that would be His best presence. (*The Subjective Experience of the Indwelling Christ*, pp. 32-33)

Further Reading: The Subjective Experience of the Indwelling Christ,
  chs. 4-5

Enlightenment and inspiration: _____

Morning Nourishment

John
14:17-18

Even the Spirit of reality, whom the world cannot receive, because it does not behold Him or know *Him; but* you know Him, because He abides with you and shall be in you. I will not leave you *as* orphans; I am coming to you.

The most precious result of our faith in Christ is that we receive Him into us. Although this is the pure and unadulterated yet mystical truth, it has been neglected by most Christians. They say that today Christ is sitting on the throne in heaven and that He does not dwell in His believers. The Bible tells us, however, that today Christ is in heaven on the right hand of God, but at the same time He also dwells in His believers (Rom. 8:34, 10). Our experience also confirms that Christ is indeed in us today. In those days the Lord Jesus was with His disciples, and He walked, stayed, and lived with them, but He could not enter into them. Therefore, He had to go and have a change through death and resurrection; in His resurrection He would come back to enter into His disciples.

The Comforter who was formerly outside the disciples could now enter into them to be the Comforter within them through the process of death and resurrection. (*The Subjective Experience of the Indwelling Christ,* pp. 33-35)

Today's Reading

First, John 14:17 says, "He abides with you," and then verse 18 says, "I will not leave you." The subject is changed from *He* to *I.* This means that *He* is *I.* "I will not leave you as orphans; I am coming to you." This coming is the coming of the Spirit of reality. The Spirit's coming is the Lord's coming. Moreover, verse 19 says, "Yet a little while and the world beholds Me no longer, but you behold Me; because I live, you also shall live." The Lord was going to die and be buried, so the world would behold Him no longer. However, the disciples beheld Him because He was resurrected. After His resurrection, He became the Spirit to enter into the disciples and live in them. Therefore, just as He lived, so they also lived. They lived together with Him. (*The Subjective Experience of the Indwelling Christ,* p. 36)

In resurrection Christ came to the disciples and breathed Himself as the Holy Spirit into them. "He breathed into them and said to them, Receive the Holy Spirit" (John 20:22)....[This] was a great work accomplished by Christ in His resurrection. The Holy Spirit is the realization of the resurrected Christ, and the Lord breathed this realization into the disciples.

Before His death and resurrection, the Lord Jesus could not be in His disciples. He could only be among them. In order to come into them, He needed to do the marvelous work of becoming the life-giving Spirit and of breathing this Spirit into the disciples. This great work was accomplished by Christ in His resurrection.

The Gospel of John reveals that Christ is the Word, the eternal God (1:1), who passed through a long process eventually to become the breath, the pneuma, that He might enter into the believers. For the accomplishment of God's eternal purpose, He took two steps. First, He took the step of incarnation to become a man in the flesh (1:14), to be the Lamb of God to accomplish redemption for man (1:29), to declare God to man (1:18), and to manifest the Father to His believers (14:9-11). Second, He took the step of death and resurrection to be transfigured into the Spirit that He might impart Himself into His believers as their life and their everything for the building of His Body, the church, the habitation of God, to express the Triune God for eternity. The Gospel of John clearly reveals that Christ became flesh to be the Lamb of God and that in resurrection He became the life-giving Spirit. Thus, in the evening of the day of His resurrection He came and breathed Himself as the Spirit into the disciples.

The Holy Spirit in John 20:22 is the Spirit expected in 7:39 and promised in 14:16-17, 26; 15:26; and 16:7-8, 13. This indicates that the Lord's breathing of the Holy Spirit into the disciples was the fulfillment of His promise of the Holy Spirit as the Comforter. (*The Conclusion of the New Testament*, pp. 799-800)

Further Reading: The Subjective Experience of the Indwelling Christ, ch. 3; *The Indwelling Christ in the Canon of the New Testament*, ch. 7

Enlightenment and inspiration: _____

_____

_____

Morning Nourishment

1 Tim. ...I was shown mercy, that in me, the foremost, Jesus
1:16 Christ might display <u>all His long-suffering</u> for a pattern
to those who are to <u>believe on Him</u> unto eternal life.
Gal. But when it pleased God, who set me apart from my
1:15-16 mother's womb and called me through His grace, to
reveal His Son in me...

The gospel of God, as the subject of Romans, concerns Christ as
the Spirit living within the believers after His resurrection. This is
higher and more subjective than what was presented in the Gospels, which concern Christ only in the flesh as He lived among His
disciples after His incarnation but before His death and resurrection. This book, however, reveals that Christ has resurrected and
has become the life-giving Spirit (8:9-10). He is no longer merely
the Christ outside the believers, but He is now the Christ within
them. Hence, the gospel in this book is the gospel of the One who is
now indwelling His believers as their subjective Savior. (*Crystalli-
zation-study of the Complete Salvation of God in Romans*, p. 9)

Today's Reading

We should not hold the concept that we cannot be an apostle
like Paul. The apostles are examples of what all believers should
be. Paul was not an extraordinary person, and he did not reach a
state that no one else can attain. The concept that the apostles are
unique is a Roman Catholic tradition. This tradition is related to
the concept that Peter was the unique successor of Christ....Far
from being unique, Peter is an example of one who followed the
Lord. In particular, he is an example to Jewish believers in Christ.
Paul is a pattern especially for Gentile believers. In 1 Timothy 1:16
he says, "...I was shown mercy, that in me, the foremost [sinner],
Jesus Christ might display all His long-suffering for a pattern to
those who are to believe on Him unto eternal life." Since Paul is
our pattern, none of us should say that we cannot be like him.

In Galatians 1:15 and 16 Paul says that God was pleased to
reveal His Son in him. The Son of God was unveiled to Paul and
shown to him. This means that he received a vision of the living

person of the Son of God. Since Paul is a pattern of the believers and the Son of God was revealed in him, we also should have Christ revealed in us. When the Son of God is revealed in us, something divine is added to us. Selection and calling do not cause anything to be added into us. But the revelation of the Son of God in us causes divinity to be added to our humanity. God Himself is added into our being to become our life. He who has the Son has life (1 John 5:12). Hence, to have the Son of God revealed in us means to have God added to us to become our life.

In Galatians 1:15 and 16 Paul says that it pleased God to reveal His Son in him. This indicates that to reveal the Son of God brings pleasure to God. Nothing is more pleasing to God than the unveiling, the revelation, of the living person of the Son of God.

The more revelation we receive of the Son of God, the more He will live in us. The more He lives in us, the more He will become to us the unique and central blessing of the gospel which God promised to Abraham. This means that He will be to us the all-inclusive land realized as the all-inclusive, processed, life-giving Spirit. This should not simply be a doctrine to us. If we drop our concepts, turn our heart to the Lord, pay attention to the spirit, and spend time in the Word, Christ will be revealed in us, He will live in us, and He will be formed in us. Day by day, He will become more of an enjoyment to us. As a result, this living person will make us a new creation in a practical way. The book of Galatians eventually brings us to the new creation by way of the inward revelation of the living person of the Son of God.

Paul's burden in writing the book of Galatians, and our need today, is that we be brought into a state where we are full of the revelation of the Son of God and thereby become a new creation with Christ living in us, being formed in us, and being enjoyed by us continually as the all-inclusive Spirit. (*Life-study of Galatians*, pp. 41, 45, 38-40)

Further Reading: Life-study of Galatians, msgs. 4-5; *The Indwelling Christ in the Canon of the New Testament,* ch. 11

Enlightenment and inspiration: _____

_____

_____

_____

Morning Nourishment

Gal. For as many of you as were baptized into Christ have
3:27 put on Christ.
4:19 My children, with whom I travail again in birth until
Christ is formed in you.

In John 6:57 the Lord Jesus said, "As the living Father has sent Me and I live because of the Father, so he who eats Me, he also shall live because of Me." The Son did not live by Himself. However, this does not mean that the Son was set aside and ceased to exist. The Son, of course, continued to exist, but He did not live His own life. Instead, He lived the life of the Father. In this way the Son and the Father had one life and one living. They shared the same life and had the same living.

It is the same in our relationship with Christ today. We and Christ do not have two lives. Rather, we have one life and one living. We live by Him, and He lives in us. If we do not live, He does not live; and if He does not live, we cannot live. On the one hand, we are terminated; on the other hand, we continue to exist, but we do not live without Him. Christ lives within us, and we live with Him. Therefore, we and He have one life and one living. (*Life-study of Galatians*, pp. 88-89)

Today's Reading

"I," the natural person, is inclined to keep the law that I might be perfect (Phil. 3:6), but God wants me to live Christ that God may be expressed in me through Him (Phil. 1:20-21). Hence, God's economy is that "I" be crucified in Christ's death and Christ live in me in His resurrection. To keep the law is to exalt it above all things in my life; to live Christ is to make Him the center in my life, even to make Him everything to me. The law was used by God to keep His chosen people in custody for Christ for a period of time (Gal. 3:23), and eventually to conduct them to Christ (3:24) that they might receive Him as life and live Him as God's expression. Since Christ has come, the function of the law has been terminated; therefore, Christ must replace the law in my life for the fulfillment of God's eternal purpose.

To have Christ formed in us is to have Christ grown in us in full. First Christ was born into us at our conversion, then He lives in us in our Christian life (2:20), and He will be formed in us at our maturity [4:19]. This is needed that we may be sons of full age, heirs to inherit God's promised blessing, and mature in the divine sonship.

In Galatians 3:27 Paul says that as many as are baptized into Christ have put on Christ. To put on Christ is to clothe ourselves with Christ, to put on Christ as a garment. On the one hand, in baptism we are immersed into Christ; on the other hand, in baptism we put on Christ. Christ, the living Spirit, is the water of life. Hence, to be baptized into Christ is to be immersed into Him as the Spirit. When a person is immersed into Christ, he automatically puts on Christ as his clothing. This means that the baptized one has become one with Christ, having been immersed into Him and having become clothed with Him.

If Christ were not the life-giving Spirit, there would be no way for us to be baptized into Christ. How could we be baptized into Christ if, according to the traditional teaching of the Trinity, He were only sitting in the heavens? For us to be baptized into Christ, Christ must be the *pneuma*, the air, the Spirit all around us....We cannot be baptized into a Christ who is only in the heavens. But we can be baptized into the Christ who is the *pneuma*, the Spirit. This is proved by 1 Corinthians 12:13, where we are told that in one Spirit we were baptized into one Body. The Spirit here is the all-inclusive, processed Triune God. In the Spirit, the processed Triune God, we have been baptized into one Body. Therefore, for us to be baptized into such a divine reality, Christ must be the life-giving Spirit. Whenever we baptize others, we should tell them that the Triune God as the processed life-giving Spirit is all around them, and that they need to be baptized, immersed, into the reality of this divine person. (*Life-study of Galatians*, pp. 89, 205, 184-185)

Further Reading: Life-study of Galatians, msgs. 10, 21, 23; *The Indwelling Christ in the Canon of the New Testament*, ch. 12

Enlightenment and inspiration: _____

_____

_____

_____

Morning Nourishment

Eph. That He would grant you, according to the riches of
3:16-17 His glory, to be strengthened with power through His
Spirit into the inner man, that Christ may make His
home in your hearts through faith...
Phil. For God is my witness how I long after you all in the
1:8 inward parts of Christ Jesus.

God the Father is exercising His authority through God the
Spirit to strengthen us into the inner man that God the Son may
make His home deep down in our hearts. I am sorry to say that
some Christians even argue that Christ is not in us. They say that
Christ is merely on the throne,...that Christ is too great to enter
into us small human beings. We all need to declare, however, that
the Bible teaches that Christ is not only in us (Col. 1:27) but that
He is also making His home downward in our heart. He is housing
Himself in our heart. (*God's New Testament Economy,* pp. 404-405)

Today's Reading

The apostle Paul prayed for us that our inner man might be
made strong. The result, then, is that Christ will spread within
our heart. For Christ to make His home in our heart means that
He will saturate and permeate every part of our heart with Himself. Then our whole being will be a home to Him, and He will be
the dweller. He will not only be our life, but the living person who
is the dweller of our being.

According to God's economy, the Body of Christ must have a
living person who is so real, practical, living, and available. This is
why God's intention is that Christ make His home in us. It is not a
matter of whether we are right or wrong; it is a matter of having
Christ as a living person spreading into our whole being. We
should not try to be right, but rather practice taking Christ as our
person. If He is making His home in our heart, then we are hitting
the mark. The problem is that we try to be so right, yet we do not
have Christ making His home in our heart....The central point in
Ephesians is Christ making His home in our heart. This is the
way we can participate in all the unsearchable riches of Christ.

The practical experience of the indwelling Christ is to let Him make His home in our heart. It is not my doing, it is not my behaving, it is altogether my letting Him make His home in me. All day long we must learn to say, "Lord Jesus, I take You as my person." Then He will take over every part of our being, and our heart will become His home. (*The Indwelling Christ in the Canon of the New Testament,* pp. 119-120)

In Philippians 1:8 Paul went on to say, "For God is my witness how I long after you all in the inward parts of Christ Jesus." This verse indicates that Paul experienced the inward parts of Christ. The Greek word rendered "inward parts" means bowels. It signifies inward affection, then tender mercy and sympathy. Paul was one with Christ even in His bowels, the tender inward parts, in longing after the saints.

Verses 7 and 8 belong together and should not be separated. Notice that verse 8 begins with the conjunction "for." This indicates that grace is related to the inward parts of Christ. Paul partook of grace, for he longed after all the saints in the inward parts of Christ. To enjoy Christ is to be one in Christ's inward parts. This refers not only to enjoyment, but also to living Christ. To live Christ is to abide in His inward parts and there to enjoy Him as grace.

Elsewhere in this chapter Paul speaks of magnifying Christ and living Christ. Experientially, to magnify Christ and to live Christ require that we remain in the inward parts of Christ. In simple words, this is to abide in Him. If we would be those in Christ, we must be in His inward parts. We need to be in His tender heart and delicate feelings. If we abide here, we shall enjoy Christ as grace and experience Him in a very practical way. As we experience Christ and enjoy Him as our grace, we shall be sustained in suffering for the gospel by caring for the accomplishment of God's economy on earth today. (*Life-study of Philippians,* pp. 29-30)

Further Reading: The Indwelling Christ in the Canon of the New Testament, chs. 13-15; Life-study of Philippians, msg. 3

Enlightenment and inspiration: _____

_____

_____

_____

Morning Nourishment

Phil. Let this mind be in you, which was also in Christ
2:5   Jesus.
2 Cor. But whom you forgive anything, I also *forgive;* for
2:10   also what I have forgiven, if I have forgiven any-
        thing, *it is* for your sake in the person of Christ.

In Philippians 2, Paul tells us that we must have the mind of
Christ. "Let this mind be in you, which was also in Christ Jesus"
(Phil. 2:5). This corresponds to that which is mentioned in Romans
12:2. There we see that we must be transformed by the renewing
of our mind. This means that our mind is replaced with the mind
of Christ. In other words, we must take the person of Christ. We
must put our mind aside, and take the mind of Christ. This is a
kind of substitution. We reject our own person, and take Christ as
our person. Therefore, His mind becomes our mind. (*The Indwelling Christ in the Canon of the New Testament,* p. 135)

Today's Reading

If we love [the Lord] and cooperate with Him, we afford Him
the opportunity to come into our mind to become its content. This
is just like the thumb of our hand getting into the thumb of a glove
to be its content. You have believed in the Lord, yet your mind
may be void of Christ…[and] filled with your children and spouse
and your property. In your mind there is no Christ; rather, there
are just yourself and things that are outside of Christ. You have
shut Christ outside the door of your mind. Therefore, although He
is in your spirit, He is suffering because He cannot get into your
mind. This is the real situation of many among us.

If you love the Lord, you should say, "O Lord, I want to take
Your mind as my mind. Now I am thinking about my spouse, my
children, my studies, and my work. Lord, I don't want to consider
them according to my mind. I want You to come into my mind to
be its contents so that I may think according to Your mind." This
is to live Christ. To begin living Christ is to let the mind of Christ
be your mind and consider everything that is related to you,
including any person, matter, and thing, according to the mind of

Christ. In this way Christ can enter and occupy your mind, and you can take His mind as your mind. (*The Subjective Experience of the Indwelling Christ*, p. 51)

Second Corinthians 1:1 through 2:11...is a long introduction to this Epistle....Paul received information (7:6-13) that they had accepted his rebukes in the first Epistle, and that they had repented. This information caused him to be comforted and encouraged. Thus, he writes this Epistle to comfort and encourage them in a very personal, tender, and affectionate way, so much so that this Epistle may be considered to some extent his autobiography. In it we see a person who lives Christ, according to what he wrote concerning Him in his first Epistle, in the closest and most intimate contact with Him, acting according to the index of His eyes; a person who is one with Christ, full of Christ, and is saturated with Christ; one who is broken and even terminated in his natural life, softened and flexible in his will, affectionate yet restricted in his emotion, considerate and sober in his mind, and pure and genuine in his spirit toward the believers for their benefit, that they may experience and enjoy Christ as he does for the fulfillment of God's eternal purpose in the building up of Christ's Body.

We have pointed out that the word "person" here denotes that part of the face around the eyes, that part which is the index of a person's thoughts and feelings and which thereby signifies the presentation of the whole person. If you want to know how someone feels toward you, whether he is happy or sad, satisfied or dissatisfied, you do not look at his face in a general way, but at that part around the eyes, which is the index of the person's thoughts and feelings.

Paul lived in the closest and most intimate contact with Christ, acting according to the index of His eyes. He was truly a person who was one with Christ, full of Christ, and saturated with Christ. (*Life-study of 2 Corinthians*, pp. 32-34)

Further Reading: The Indwelling Christ in the Canon of the New Testament, chs. 8-10; *Life-study of 2 Corinthians*, msg. 4

Enlightenment and inspiration: _____

_____

_____

_____

948:
(Glory, glory, Christ is life in me)

Hymns, #538

1   It is God's intent and pleasure
     To have Christ revealed in me;
   Nothing outward as religion,
     But His Christ within to be.

     It is God's intent and pleasure
       That His Christ be wrought in me;
     Nothing outwardly performing,
       But His Christ my all to be.

2   It is God's intent and pleasure
     That His Christ may live in me;
   Nothing as an outward practise,
     But Christ working inwardly.

3   It is God's intent and pleasure
     That His Christ be formed in me;
   Not the outward forms to follow,
     But Christ growing inwardly.

4   It is God's intent and pleasure
     That His Christ make home in me;
   Not just outwardly to serve Him,
     But Christ dwelling inwardly.

5   It is God's intent and pleasure
     That His Christ my hope may be;
   It is not objective glory,
     But 'tis Christ subjectively.

6   It is God's intent and pleasure
     That His Christ be all in me;
   Nothing outwardly possessing,
     But His Christ eternally.

Composition for prophecy with main point and sub-points: _____
_____
_____
_____
_____
_____
_____
_____
_____
_____
_____
_____
_____
_____
_____
_____
_____
_____
_____
_____
_____
_____
_____
_____
_____
_____
_____
_____
_____
_____
_____
_____
_____
_____
_____
_____
_____

The Spirit

Scripture Reading: John 7:37-39; 1 Cor. 15:45b; Rom. 8:16; 1 Cor. 6:17; Rev. 1:4; 4:5; 5:6; 22:17a

Day 1

I. The Spirit of God moved in God's creation of the universe (Gen. 1:2).

II. The Spirit of Jehovah acted in God's reaching of men and in His care for men (Judg. 3:10; 6:34; Gen. 6:3a).

III. The Spirit of holiness was for God's making His chosen people holy unto Himself (Psa. 51:11; Isa. 63:10-11).

IV. The Spirit was the Holy Spirit in the conception of John the Baptist to introduce God's becoming a man in His incarnation (Luke 1:13-17) and in the conception of Jesus in God's incarnation to be a man in the flesh (vv. 30-36; Matt. 1:18-20).

Day 2

V. The Spirit was the Spirit with whom Jesus was anointed and who was in the move of the man Jesus in His ministry to God on the earth (Mark 1:10, 12; Matt. 4:1; Luke 4:1, 18; John 1:32-33).

VI. The Spirit was there to anoint and to move with Christ, but at that time the Spirit had not yet entered into the believers to flow out as rivers of living water; in this sense, the Spirit was not yet, because by that time Jesus had not yet been glorified in His resurrection (7:37-39; Luke 24:26).

VII. Through and in His resurrection Christ as the last Adam became the life-giving Spirit to enter into His believers to flow out as rivers of living water (1 Cor. 15:45b; Rev. 21:6; 22:17c):

Day 3

A. The life-giving Spirit as the Spirit of Jesus is concerning Jesus in His humanity, who passed through human living and death on the cross, indicating that in the Spirit there are not only the divine element of God but also the human element

of Jesus and the elements of His human living
and of His suffering of death as well (Acts 16:7).

B. The life-giving Spirit as the Spirit of Christ is
concerning Christ in His divinity, who conquered
death and became the life in resurrection with
the resurrection power, indicating that in the
Spirit there is the element of divinity that became the death-conquering and life-dispensing
Spirit (Rom. 8:9b).

C. The life-giving Spirit as the Spirit of Jesus Christ
comprises all the elements of Jesus' humanity
with His death and Christ's divinity with His
resurrection, which become the bountiful supply
of the unsearchable Christ for the support of His
believers (Phil. 1:19b).

D. The life-giving Spirit as the Lord Spirit, the pneumatic Christ, is for the metabolic transformation
of the believers into the Lord's image from glory to
glory by the renewing of the mind (2 Cor. 3:17-18;
Rom. 12:2b) and is for the growth and the building up of the Body of Christ (1 Cor. 3:6, 9b, 12a;
Eph. 4:16b).

E. When the man Jesus became the life-giving Spirit,
the Triune God was fully completed, consummated:

1. The Triune God was consummated in Christ's
resurrection, so after His resurrection, the
Lord came back to say that we are to baptize
people into the name of the Father and of the
Son and of the Holy Spirit (Matt. 28:19b).

2. The Triune God has been consummated in
the life-giving Spirit, the Spirit of Jesus, the
Spirit of Christ, the Spirit of Jesus Christ,
and the Lord Spirit, so this Spirit today is
the consummation of the Triune God.

F. The life-giving Spirit as the consummation of the
processed Triune God is the Paraclete, the Comforter, to the believers (John 14:16-17).

G. The life-giving Spirit is the reality of the processed
Triune God (v. 17a; 15:26b; 16:13; 1 John 5:6b).

Entering Sp   Good peas no way to reach us.

H. The life-giving Spirit is the reaching of the processed Triune God to the believers.

I. The life-giving Spirit is the believers' access unto the Father, the source of the Divine Trinity (Eph. 2:18).

We enter into Him
& enjoy the fellowship

J. The life-giving Spirit is the fellowship of the processed Triune God with the believers for their enjoyment of the riches of the Divine Trinity (2 Cor. 13:14).

(Korean)

Day 4 **VIII. The Spirit is the compound anointing Spirit (Exo. 30:22-30):**

a marvellous type

olive oil & 4 spices

A. The Spirit is compounded with the unique God as the base, as the divinity of Christ, typified by the one hin of olive oil (v. 24b).

eg. death & resur of Christ
→ all in this Sp.

B. The Spirit is compounded with God's Divine Trinity, typified by the three units of five hundred shekels of the spices (vv. 23-24a).

Andrew Murray
(1828-1917)

"in spirit of Glorified Jesus"

C. The Spirit is compounded with Christ's humanity, typified by the four kinds of spices.

D. The Spirit is compounded with Christ's death and its killing effectiveness, typified by myrrh and cinnamon (v. 23a).

E. The Spirit is compounded with Christ's resurrection and its repelling power, typified by calamus and cassia (vv. 23b-24a).

anoint tabernacle /
Ark, holy place,
making holy ~
altar / ~

Te persons & sons

F. All the above elements compounded together create an ointment for the anointing of all the things and persons related to the worship of God (vv. 25-30; 2 Cor. 1:21; 1 John 2:20, 27).

G. The compound anointing Spirit operates as the Holy Spirit to seal the believers of Christ (Eph. 1:13; 4:30b; 2 Cor. 1:22a).

we are saturated
w/ Spirit
& transformed
& become
treasure of God

H. The sealing Spirit becomes a pledge to the believers, guaranteeing God as the inheritance of the believers and giving them a foretaste of God as their heritage (Eph. 1:14; 2 Cor. 1:22b).

Day 5 **IX. The Spirit is the blessing of the gospel (Gal. 3:8, 14):**   *As ~*

A. The Spirit regenerates the believers, begetting

Abraham receive the bless — & this blessg is Just the Spirit them as the many sons of God (John 3:5-6).

B. The Spirit is the Spirit of the Son to cry, "Abba, Father!" in the believers' hearts and to lead the believers to walk as the sons of God (Gal. 4:6; Rom. 8:14-16).

C. The Spirit is for the priesthood of the gospel to sanctify the believers (15:16).

D. The Spirit intercedes for the believers (8:26).

E. The Spirit renews the believers, making them the new creation of God (Titus 3:5b; 2 Cor. 5:17).

X. **The seven Spirits are the sevenfold intensi-fied Spirit for the church's degradation in the dark age; in Revelation 1 the sevenfold Spirit is ranked as the second in the Divine Trinity instead of the third, indicating the intensifi-cation of the Spirit (vv. 4-5a):**

A. The seven Spirits are the seven lamps of fire burning before the throne of God to carry out the divine administration for the consummation of the divine economy (4:5).

B. The seven Spirits are the seven eyes of the Lamb, the observing parts of our Redeemer, to observe all the churches in all the nations and to trans-fuse all His riches into us for the building up of His Body to consummate the building up of the New Jerusalem, thus accomplishing the eternal economy of God (5:6; 21:1-3).

C. The sevenfold intensified Spirit is the speaking Spirit to all the churches (2:7, 11, 17, 29; 3:6, 13, 22).

Day 6 XI. **The Spirit is the essential Spirit and the eco-nomical Spirit of the processed Triune God:**

A. The essential Spirit of God, the Spirit of life, was breathed into the believers as the divine essence of the divine life (John 20:22).

B. The economical Spirit of God, the Spirit of power, was poured out upon the believers as the divine essence of the divine power (Acts 1:8; 2:2, 4, 17).

XII. **The Spirit is the consummation of the proc-essed Triune God:**

A. The Spirit and the bride speak together as a universal couple (Rev. 22:17a).

B. The processed and consummated Triune God marries the redeemed, regenerated, and transformed tripartite people for His final manifestation and ultimate expression in glory for eternity (21:1—22:5).

XIII. The key to our meaning and to the meaning of the universe is in God's existence as the Spirit and also in our having a spirit; without God being the Spirit and without us having a spirit to contact God, to be one with God, the whole universe is empty, and we are nothing (John 3:6; 4:24; Rom. 8:16; 1 Cor. 6:17):

A. The spirit of man was created by God, in a particular sense, to complete God's purpose in the creation of the heavens and the earth (Gen. 2:7; Zech. 12:1; Isa. 42:5; Job 32:8).

B. Man's spirit is his inward organ for him to contact God, receive God, contain God, and assimilate God into his entire being as his life and everything (Gen. 2:7; cf. Prov. 20:27).

C. God is Spirit for man to contact Him and receive Him, and man has a spirit to contact God and contain God so that God and man may have an organic union (John 4:24; 1 John 4:13; 2 Tim. 4:22a; 1 Cor. 6:17).

D. Our spirit is the destination of the "journeying" Triune God (John 1:1; 4:24; Rom. 8:16).

E. It is in our spirit that we are regenerated (John 3:6), it is in our spirit that the Holy Spirit dwells and works (Rom. 8:16), and it is in our spirit that we enjoy Christ and His grace (2 Tim. 4:22; Gal. 6:18).

F. Man's spirit is distinct from his soul (Heb. 4:12; 1 Thes. 5:23a).

G. Our spirit is composed of the conscience (Rom. 9:1; cf. 8:16), the fellowship (John 4:24; Rom. 1:9; Luke 1:47), and the intuition (1 Cor. 2:11; Mark 2:8).

H. To exercise ourselves unto godliness is to exercise our spirit to live Christ as the Spirit in our daily life (1 Tim. 4:7):

1. We need to fan our spirit into flame (2 Tim. 1:6-7).
2. We need to set our mind on our spirit (Rom. 8:6).
3. We need to discern our spirit from our soul (Heb. 4:12).

I. The Lord is with our spirit so that we may enjoy Him as grace in order to stand against the downward current of the church's decline and to carry out God's economy through His indwelling Spirit and equipping word (2 Tim. 4:22; 1:14; 3:16-17).

Morning Nourishment

Gen. ...The Spirit of God was brooding upon the surface of
1:2 the waters.
Matt. ...Behold, an angel of the Lord appeared to him in a
1:20 dream, saying, Joseph, son of David, do not be afraid
to take Mary your wife, for that which has been begotten in her is of the Holy Spirit.

In the Old Testament, the Spirit is the Spirit of God, the Spirit
of Jehovah, and the Spirit of holiness.
Genesis 1:1 says that in the beginning God created the heavens
and the earth. Then the following verse says, "The Spirit of God
was brooding upon the surface of the waters." Thus, we see that
the Spirit was the Spirit of God in God's creation of the universe.
After His creation, God began to work on man. In God's work
on man, His name is *Jehovah*. The Spirit of Jehovah is in God's
reaching of men and in His care for men (Judg. 3:10; 6:34; Gen.
6:3a). (*The Spirit with Our Spirit*, p. 19)

Today's Reading

God is caring for man mainly to make man holy. To be holy
means to be separated unto God. Man's fall caused him to depart
from God to become common, worldly, secular, and even dirty.
So God needs to take care of man, making man separate from
all things other than Himself. This is to make man holy. Thus,
the Spirit in the Old Testament is the Spirit of holiness in God's
making His chosen people holy unto Himself (Psa. 51:11; Isa.
63:10-11). This is not the same as *the Holy Spirit,* which is used in
the New Testament. The Holy Spirit is more intensified than the
Spirit of holiness.
In the New Testament, the revelation concerning the Spirit is
more complicated....The first divine title used for the Spirit in the
New Testament is *the Holy Spirit.* According to the Greek text,
the title translated as *the Holy Spirit* may be in two forms: *the
Spirit the Holy* or *the Holy Spirit.* According to my understanding,
this means that in the New Testament age, the very God who
is the Spirit is "the Holy." God is a Spirit and this Spirit now is

totally "the Holy." We are now in an age in which God Himself as the Spirit is "the Holy" to make man not only separated unto Him but also one with Him. In the Old Testament, the most God could do with man was to make man separated unto Him but not one with Him. But now in the New Testament age, the time has come in which God would go further and deeper to make man absolutely one with Him, to make man Him and to make Him man. Athanasius, who was one of the church fathers, said concerning Christ: "He was made man that we might be made God." This means that we are made God in life and in nature, but not in the Godhead. This process takes place by *the Spirit the Holy*.

The beginning of the New Testament gives a record of two conceptions. One was the conception of John the Baptist [Luke 1:13-17] and the other was the conception of the Lord Jesus in God's incarnation to be a man in the flesh (Luke 1:30-36; Matt. 1:18-20). With these two conceptions, the New Testament uses the particular title *the Holy Spirit*. *The Holy Spirit* is used in the New Testament due to the change of the age. In order for God to become a man so that man could become God, there was the need of the Holy Spirit.

We need to see that the conception of John the Baptist was strikingly different in essance from that of Jesus the Savior. With John's conception, the essence of the Holy Spirit was not involved but the power. The conception of John was by the power of the Holy Spirit through man's instrument. But with the conception of Jesus, the very essence of the Holy Spirit Himself was involved [Matt. 1:20]....The conception of the Savior was God's incarnation (John 1:14), constituted...of the divine essence added to the human essence, thus producing the God-man of two natures—divinity and humanity. These two conceptions are related to the beginning of God making Himself man and of God making man Him that He might become man and man might become Him, that the two could be one entity. (*The Spirit with Our Spirit*, pp. 20-23)

Further Reading: The Spirit with Our Spirit, ch. 1

Enlightenment and inspiration: _____

_____

_____

_____

Morning Nourishment

Luke **And Jesus, full of the Holy Spirit, returned from the**
4:1 **Jordan and was led by the Spirit…**
18 **"The Spirit of the Lord is upon Me…"**
John **He who believes into Me…out of his innermost being**
7:38-39 **shall flow rivers of living water. But this He said concerning the Spirit, whom those who believed into Him were about to receive; for *the* Spirit was not yet, because Jesus had not yet been glorified.**

The Spirit anointed Jesus and was in the move of the man Jesus in His ministry to God on the earth (Mark 1:10, 12; Matt. 4:1; Luke 4:1, 18; John 1:32-33). After Jesus was baptized,…the Spirit as the dove came upon Jesus as the Lamb to carry out God's redemption and salvation for the accomplishing of God's economy.

Luke 4 says that the coming down of the dove upon the man Jesus was the anointing (vv. 1, 18)….This anointing made Jesus a particular man. In the Old Testament, a number of people were anointed with oil, and then the Spirit came down to reach the anointed one (Exo. 29:7; 1 Sam. 9:16; 16:12; 1 Kings 1:34; 19:15-16). But the anointed one was not anointed with the Spirit directly. In the New Testament, however, Jesus was anointed directly with the Spirit as a dove.

In [the] Gospels we see that…the anointing God is one with the anointed man. The dove was in the air. The Lamb was on the earth. But now here is one entity—the dove on the Lamb. The One in the air is now one with the One on the earth. God and man have become one, indicating a kind of organic union. The anointing Spirit and the man Jesus became one in His ministry. (*The Spirit with Our Spirit*, pp. 23-24)

Today's Reading

[In the Gospels] the Spirit was there to anoint Christ and to move with Christ, but at that time the Spirit had not yet entered into the believers to flow out as rivers of living water (John 7:37-39). …John 7 tells us that the Spirit was not yet, because by that time Jesus was not glorified in His resurrection. Resurrection was for the man Jesus to get out of His human shell and to release the divine life, and this resurrection is called glorification. Before Christ was thus glorified, the Spirit was not yet. When John said "the Spirit was not yet," he meant that the Spirit was not yet to flow out of the believers as rivers of living water. But the Spirit was there for the anointing of Christ and the moving of Christ in His ministry.

The anointing of Jesus the man and the moving with Jesus the man was God making Himself one with man on a small scale in an individual way, with one person. But when the Spirit flows into the believers and flows out of them as many rivers of living water, God being one with man and man being one with God becomes a corporate matter. It is not just with one man, Jesus, but with millions of His believers. This is the enlargement of God being one with man. God's being one with man altogether depends upon the Spirit. The Spirit is a big key to the organic union of God with man.

Through and in His resurrection Christ as the last Adam became the life-giving Spirit to enter into His believers to flow out as rivers of living water (1 Cor. 15:45b; Rev. 21:6; 22:17c). God is a Spirit and the second of the Triune God in the flesh became a life-giving Spirit. Prior to Christ's resurrection, God was a Spirit but not a life-giving Spirit. Before Christ's death and resurrection, God had no way to enter into man to be man's life. Between man and God there were a number of negative things as obstacles.

In His death He fulfilled all the requirements of God's glory, holiness, and righteousness; then in resurrection He changed in form to be the life-giving Spirit. This was absolutely for the organic union between God and man—to bring God into man and to bring man into God in His resurrection. Today we can take the tree of life and drink the water of life so that the Triune God can flow out from our innermost being as rivers of living water. (*The Spirit with Our Spirit,* pp. 24-26)

Further Reading: The Spirit with Our Spirit, ch. 2

Enlightenment and inspiration: _____

_____

_____

_____

Morning Nourishment

Acts ...When they had come to Mysia, they tried to go into
16:7 Bithynia, yet the Spirit of Jesus did not allow them.
Rom. ...Yet if anyone does not have the Spirit of Christ, he is
8:9 not of Him.
Phil. For I know that for me this will turn out to salvation
1:19 through your petition and *the* bountiful supply of the
Spirit of Jesus Christ.

In the New Testament, the life-giving Spirit is referred to as the Spirit of Jesus (Acts 16:7). This title of the Spirit is concerning Jesus in His humanity, who passed through human living and death on the cross. It indicates that in the Spirit there is not only the divine element of God but also the human element of Jesus and the elements of His human living and suffering of death.

The Spirit of Christ is concerning Christ in His divinity, who conquered death and became the life in resurrection with the resurrection power, indicating that in the Spirit there is the element of divinity that became the death-conquering and the life-dispensing Spirit (Rom. 8:9b).

The Spirit of Jesus Christ refers to the Spirit, comprising all the elements of Jesus' humanity with His death and Christ's divinity with His resurrection, who becomes the bountiful supply of the unsearchable Christ for the support of His believers (Phil. 1:19b). (*The Spirit with Our Spirit,* p. 31)

Today's Reading

The Lord Spirit is a compound title (2 Cor. 3:18) referring to the pneumatic Christ....The Lord Spirit, the pneumatic Christ, is for the metabolic transformation of the believers into the Lord's image, from one degree of glory to a higher degree of glory (2 Cor. 3:17-18). Such transformation takes place by the renewing of the mind (Rom. 12:2b), and this is for the growth and the building up of the Body of Christ (1 Cor. 3:6, 9b, 12a; Eph. 4:16b).

It is difficult to see in the Old Testament that the Triune God is the Father, the Son, and the Holy Spirit. It is not until the end of the first Gospel in the New Testament that we see the composition of the Divine Trinity (Matt. 28:19b)....After [Christ's] resurrection, and before His ascension, He came back to the disciples and charged them to disciple the nations, baptizing them, the new believers, into the name of the Father and of the Son and of the Holy Spirit. In the Acts the apostles baptized people into the name of Jesus Christ (8:16; 19:5). This means that Jesus Christ equals the Father, the Son, and the Spirit. Before the man Jesus became the life-giving Spirit, the Divine Trinity was not fully consummated.

The second of the Divine Trinity is the Son....Before Christ was incarnated, He did not have humanity; before His incarnation the Son was only divine. Furthermore, before His resurrection the Son was God's only begotten Son, not the Firstborn. In this sense, the second of the Divine Trinity was not fully consummated before His resurrection. He needed to pick up humanity through incarnation, and He needed to become the firstborn Son of God through resurrection (Acts 13:33). So after His incarnation and resurrection, the second of the Trinity was completed, consummated.

Now we need to consider the third of the Divine Trinity—the Spirit. Before the incarnation and resurrection, the Spirit was only the Spirit of God, not the Spirit of man. The Spirit of Jesus is the Spirit of man. In the Spirit of God prior to the incarnation, there was no human living, no all-inclusive death, and no element of resurrection. In other words, before the incarnation and the resurrection, the Spirit of God was not compounded. It was through incarnation, human living, crucifixion, and resurrection that the Spirit of God was compounded with humanity and with Christ's death and resurrection. So after Christ's resurrection, the third of the Divine Trinity was also consummated.

The Triune God has been consummated in the life-giving Spirit, the Spirit of Jesus, the Spirit of Christ, the Spirit of Jesus Christ, and the Lord Spirit. So this Spirit today is the consummation of the Triune God. (*The Spirit with Our Spirit*, pp. 32-33)

Further Reading: The Spirit with Our Spirit, ch. 3

Enlightenment and inspiration: _____

_____

_____

_____

Morning Nourishment

Exo.   **You also take the finest spices: of flowing myrrh five**
30:23-25   **hundred *shekels*, and of fragrant cinnamon half as**
much...and of fragrant calamus two hundred fifty
***shekels*, and of cassia five hundred *shekels*...and a hin**
of olive oil. And you shall make it a holy anointing oil,
a fragrant ointment compounded according to the
work of a compounder; it shall be a holy anointing oil.

The best type of the all-inclusive Spirit of Christ as the compound anointing Spirit is the compound ointment spoken of in
Exodus 30....This type reveals that the compound anointing Spirit
is compounded with the unique God, as the base, as the divinity of
Christ, typified by the one hin of olive oil (v. 24b).

The compound anointing Spirit is compounded with God's
Divine Trinity, typified by the three units of five hundred shekels
of the spices (vv. 23-24a). The middle unit of five hundred shekels was split into two units....This signifies that the second of the
Divine Trinity was split, crucified, on the cross.

The compound anointing Spirit is also compounded with Christ's
humanity, typified by the four kinds of spices.

The Spirit is compounded with Christ's death and its killing
effectiveness, typified by myrrh and cinnamon (v. 23a).

Christ's resurrection and its repelling power, typified by calamus and cassia (vv. 23b-24a), are also elements of the compound
anointing Spirit. Calamus is a reed shooting up into the air out of
a marsh or a muddy place. Thus, it signifies the rising up of the
Lord Jesus from the place of death. Cassia in ancient times was
used as a repellent to drive away insects and snakes. Thus, it signifies the repelling power of Christ's resurrection. (*The Spirit
with Our Spirit*, p. 44)

Today's Reading

All the above elements compounded together create an ointment for the anointing of all the things and persons related to the
worship of God (Exo. 30:25-30; 2 Cor. 1:21; 1 John 2:20, 27).

In the New Testament, we see the compound anointing Spirit

operating as the Holy Spirit to seal the believers of Christ (Eph. 1:13; 4:30b; 2 Cor. 1:22a). To seal means to anoint....When we live by the Spirit, we have the sense that something within us is saturating us, and that saturating is the continuous sealing. This sealing dispenses the divine element of the processed Triune God into the believers and saturates them with it. It also transforms the believers into the inheritance of God (Eph. 1:11). It is remarkable that we sinners can be transformed to such an extent that we are considered by God as His inheritance. How could we, the constitution of sin, be God's inheritance? Surely, this implies transformation.

Our being God's inheritance, as spoken of in Ephesians 1:11, is related to Christ's redemption (v. 7). We were lost in sin, but Christ's redemption brought us out of sin and unto God. Then we became persons in Christ. Christ has become our sphere and our realm in which His element is always saturating us, and that saturating is the Spirit's sealing to transform us into God's treasure,...His inheritance. The life-giving Spirit anoints us, seals us, saturates us, with the divine element. This saturating is the dispensing, and the dispensing is transforming us, making us the treasure of God. If we walk in the Spirit every day, even every moment, we are under this sealing, this saturating, to transform us into a treasure for God's inheritance.

The sealing Spirit becomes a pledge to the believers (Eph. 1:14; 2 Cor. 1:22b), guaranteeing God as the inheritance of the believers and giving the believers a foretaste of God as their heritage. We are God's inheritance, and God is our inheritance. For us to be God's inheritance, we need the sealing. For us to have God as our inheritance, we need the pledging....The Greek word for *pledge* was used in the purchasing of land. The seller gave the purchaser some soil from the land....Hence, a pledge, according to ancient Greek usage, is also a sample. The Holy Spirit is a sample of what we will inherit of God in full. (*The Spirit with Our Spirit,* pp. 45-46)

Further Reading: The Spirit with Our Spirit, ch. 4; *The Spirit of the Glorified Jesus* by Andrew Murray (booklet)

Enlightenment and inspiration: _____

_____

_____

_____

Morning Nourishment

Gal. In order that the blessing of Abraham might come to
3:14 the Gentiles in Christ Jesus, that we might receive
the promise of the Spirit through faith.

4:6 And because you are sons, God has sent forth the
Spirit of His Son into our hearts, crying, Abba, Father!

Rev. And I saw...a Lamb standing as having *just* been
5:6 slain, having seven horns and seven eyes, which are
the seven Spirits of God sent forth into all the earth.

In the New Testament, the Spirit is also revealed as the blessing of the gospel (Gal. 3:8, 14). The blessing of the gospel is the Spirit, the consummation of the Triune God. Nothing is greater than the consummated Triune God.

The Spirit regenerates the believers, begetting them as the many sons of God (John 3:5-6; Heb. 2:10)....When we cry "Abba, Father" in our spirit from our heart, that is the Spirit's crying....The Spirit is for the priesthood of the gospel to sanctify the believers (Rom. 15:16). Whenever we preach the gospel, we fulfill our priesthood of the gospel, and when we fulfill our priesthood, the Spirit goes along with us to sanctify the new believers.... According to Romans 8:26, the Spirit intercedes for the believers. This is another aspect of the Spirit as the blessing of the gospel....The Spirit also functions to renew the believers, making them the new creation of God (Titus 3:5b; 2 Cor. 5:17). Thus, we have seen the Spirit's regenerating, crying and leading, sanctifying, interceding, and renewing to make us not only the sons of God but also the new creation. Such a wonderful Spirit is the blessing of the gospel.

The Spirit is the reality of the new testament. The unique bequest of the new testament is the Spirit as the consummated Triune God. He is within us. He is sealing us, saturating us, transforming us, and causing us to walk as the sons of God to make us a new creation. (*The Spirit with Our Spirit*, pp. 46-47)

Today's Reading

The book of Revelation reveals the seven Spirits as the sevenfold intensified Spirit for the church's degradation in the dark age. Even by the end of the first century, the church had become degraded. The apostles Paul, Peter, and John all dealt with this degradation in their writings—particularly in 2 Timothy, 2 Peter, and the three Epistles of John....Because of the degradation in the dark age, God has intensified His Spirit sevenfold.

Revelation 4:5 says that the seven Spirits are the seven lamps burning before the throne of God to carry out the divine administration for the consummation of the divine economy. God's administration today is not weak. The administration of God today on this earth to accomplish His economy is strong in a sevenfold way. The sevenfold Spirit is the seven lamps of fire before the throne of God to direct the world situation in order to execute God's economy in the universe.

The seven Spirits are the seven eyes of the Lamb, the observing parts of our Redeemer, to observe all the churches in all the nations for the building up of His Body to consummate the building up of the New Jerusalem, accomplishing the eternal economy of God (Rev. 5:6; 21:1-3). Eventually, the life-giving Spirit, the compound Spirit, has become the sevenfold Spirit as the seven eyes of the Lamb. This exposes the wrong teaching that Christ and the Spirit are separate. The seven Spirits are the eyes of Christ. How could your eyes be separate from you? They are a part of you. A person's eyes are for observing and transfusing....The sevenfold Spirit today is the eyes of our Savior. He observes us and transfuses all His riches into us by His seven eyes.

The sevenfold intensified Spirit is the speaking Spirit to all the churches. The Lord's epistles to the seven churches are in Revelation 2 and 3. At the beginning of each epistle, it was the Lord Jesus speaking (2:1, 8, 12, 18; 3:1, 7, 14), yet at the end of each epistle it says that whoever has an ear should listen to what the Spirit says to all the churches (2:7, 11, 17, 29; 3:6, 13, 22). (*The Spirit with Our Spirit,* pp. 54-56)

Further Reading: The Spirit with Our Spirit, ch. 5

__Enlightenment and inspiration:__ _____

_____

_____

_____

Morning Nourishment

John **And when He had said this, He breathed into** *them*
20:22 **and said to them, Receive the Holy Spirit.**
Zech. **The burden of the word of Jehovah concerning**
12:1 **Israel.** *Thus* **declares Jehovah, who stretches forth**
the heavens and lays the foundations of the earth and
forms the spirit of man within him.

The essential Spirit of God is the Spirit of life breathed into the
believers as the divine essence of the divine life (Rom. 8:2; John
20:22). The economical Spirit of God, the Spirit of power, was
poured out upon the believers as the divine essence of the divine
power (Acts 1:8; 2:2, 4, 17). The consummated Spirit has these two
aspects: the inward, essential aspect and the outward, economical
aspect. On the day of resurrection, the Lord breathed the essential Spirit as life into His disciples. Then after fifty days, on the
day of Pentecost, He poured out the economical Spirit of power
upon the disciples. The essential Spirit is for our life and living
inwardly. The economical Spirit is for our ministry and work outwardly. To be economical means to be for God's economy, for God's
work, to carry out His plan.

Ultimately, the Spirit is the consummation of the processed
Triune God...after His ascension, that is, after He had been fully
processed. Such a Spirit speaks together with the bride as the
universal couple (Rev. 22:17a).

The conclusion of the entire...Bible reveals that the processed
and consummated Triune God marries the redeemed, regenerated, and transformed tripartite people for His final manifestation and ultimate expression in glory for eternity (Rev. 21:1—
22:5)....When Jesus came, He was God's manifestation. Then this
manifestation has an issue, and the issue is to express God. The
Triune God will have the New Jerusalem as His corporate manifestation. Then through that manifestation He will be expressed
corporately for eternity. (*The Spirit with Our Spirit,* pp. 57-58)

Today's Reading

If we did not have a spirit, we would be like the beasts. We would become meaningless. Also, if there were no God in the universe, the whole universe would become empty. So the key to our meaning and the meaning of the universe is in God's existence and also in our having a spirit. God is Spirit and we must contact Him, worship Him, in our spirit (John 4:24). These two spirits should contact each other and should become one (1 Cor. 6:17). Then the whole universe becomes meaningful. Then our life has its meaning. Without God being the Spirit and without us having a spirit to contact God, to be one with God, the whole universe is empty and we are nothing. By this we can see the importance of our spirit.

In 1 Timothy 4:7 Paul said, "Exercise yourself unto godliness." Then in verse 8 he spoke of bodily exercise....The exercise unto godliness, must be the exercise of the spirit. To exercise ourselves unto godliness is to exercise our spirit to live Christ in our daily life.

We need to fan our spirit into flame. In [2 Timothy 1:6-7] Paul said, "For which cause I remind you to fan into flame the gift of God, which is in you....For God has not given us a spirit of cowardice, but of power and of love and of sobermindedness."

After you fan your spirit into flame, learn to practice another thing. Always manage your mind....Romans 8:6 says, "The mind set on the flesh is death, but the mind set on the spirit is life and peace." After fanning our spirit into flame, we must learn to set our mind on the spirit.

The battle in the Christian life is always there. Even within us there is a battle between the spirit and the flesh and even the more between the spirit and the soul. So we have to exercise our spirit, to use our spirit, that is, to fan our spirit into flame. Then we should learn how to control our mind by setting our mind upon our spirit. We should also always discern what is of the spirit and what is of the soul. If something is not of the spirit, we do not want to say it or do it. This is to use, to exercise, our spirit. I hope we will practice using our spirit until we build up a strong habit of exercising our spirit. (*The Spirit with Our Spirit*, pp. 78, 80, 84, 86)

Further Reading: The Spirit with Our Spirit, chs. 6, 8

Enlightenment and inspiration: _____

_____

_____

_____

Hymns, #242

1 The Spirit of God today
   The Spirit of Jesus is,
   The God-man who died and rose,
   Ascending to glory His.

2 'Tis from such a Jesus came
   The Spirit of Jesus to us,
   To make His reality
   Experience unto us.

3 The Spirit of Jesus has
   All elements human, divine,
   The living of man in Him
   And glory of God combine.

4 The suff'ring of human life,
   Effectiveness of His death,
   His rising and reigning too
   Are all in the Spirit's breath.

5 With all these components true
   His Spirit in us doth move,
   And by His anointing full
   The riches of Christ we prove.

6 This Spirit of Jesus doth
   Encompass both great and small;
   Inclusively He doth work
   In us, making God our all.

Birth rights — enjoyment of Christ — —

for land, priesthood, kingship ...

Composition for prophecy with main point and sub-points: _____

_____

_____

_____

_____

_____

_____

_____

_____

_____

_____

_____

_____

_____

_____

_____

_____

_____

_____

_____

_____

_____

_____

_____

_____

_____

_____

_____

_____

_____

_____

_____

_____

_____

_____

_____

Eating the Lord as the Tree of Life and Living on the Line of Life

Scripture Reading: Gen. 2:9; John 1:4; 10:10b; 14:6a; 1 Cor. 15:45b; 2 Cor. 3:6; Rev. 2:7; 22:1-2

Day 1

I. **The tree of life signifies the Triune God embodied in Christ as life to man in the form of food (Gen. 2:9; John 1:4; 10:10b; 14:6a; 1 Cor. 15:45b; John 6:35, 57):**

A. God's placing man in front of the tree of life indicates that God wanted man to receive Him as his life by eating Him organically and assimilating Him metabolically so that God might become the very constituent of man's being (cf. 5:39-40; 2 Cor. 3:6).

B. The tree of life grows along the two sides of the river of water of life, indicating that it is a vine; since Christ is a vine tree and is also life, He is the tree of life (Rev. 2:7; 22:1-2; John 15:1; 14:6a).

C. Christ was processed through incarnation, crucifixion, and resurrection so that man might have life and live by eating Him (10:10b; 6:51, 57, 63).

Day 2

II. **We can eat the Lord as the tree of life, our spiritual food, in the following ways:**

A. We can eat Him by eating His words:

1. "Man shall not live on bread alone, but on every word that proceeds out through the mouth of God" (Matt. 4:4).

2. "How sweet are Your words to my taste! / Sweeter than honey to my mouth!" (Psa. 119:103).

3. "Then He said to me, Son of man, eat what you find; eat this scroll, and go, speak to the house of Israel. So I opened my mouth, and He gave me that scroll to eat. And He said to me, Son of man, feed your stomach and fill your inward parts with this scroll that I am giving you. And I ate it, and it was like honey in my mouth in its sweetness. Then He said to me, Son of

eat scroll → go to speak

man, go to the house of Israel and speak with My words to them" (Ezek. 3:1-4).

4. "Your words were found and I ate them, / And
lip Your word became to me / The gladness and joy of my heart, / For I am called by Your name, / O Jehovah, God of hosts" (Jer. 15:16).

5. "He who eats Me, he also shall live because
Lbk of Me...It is the Spirit who gives life; the flesh profits nothing; the words which I have spoken to you are spirit and are life" (John 6:57, 63).

B. We can eat Him by doing the will of the Father
Mtke to satisfy the hungry and thirsty ones and by glorifying the Father on earth in living the life of a God-man (Matt. 24:45-47):

Greg 1. "My food is to do the will of Him who sent Me and to finish His work" (John 4:34).

2. "I have glorified You on earth, finishing the
Frgl work which You have given Me to do" (17:4; cf. Col. 1:9-11).

Day 3   C. We can eat Him by contacting the proper people
Korean (Lev. 11:1-3, 9, 13, 21):

1. To eat is to contact things outside of us and to receive them into us, with the result that they eventually become our inner constitution.

2. In Leviticus 11 all the animals signify different kinds of people, and eating signifies our contacting of people (cf. Acts 10:9b-14, 27-29).

3. For God's people to live a holy life as required by the holy God, they must be careful about the kind of people they contact (cf. Lev. 11:46-47; 1 Cor. 15:33; 2 Cor. 6:14-18; 2 Tim. 2:22):

a. Animals that divide the hoof and chew the cud (Lev. 11:3; cf. vv. 4-8, 26-28) signify persons who have discernment in their activities (Phil. 1:9-10) and who receive the word of God with much reconsideration (Psa. 119:15).

b. Aquatic animals that have fins and scales signify persons who can move and act freely

in the world and at the same time resist its
influence (fins help fish to move, to act, in
water according to their wishes, and scales
protect the fish that live in the sea from
being salted) (Lev. 11:9).

c. Birds that have wings for flying and that
eat seeds of life as their food supply signify
persons who can live and move in a life that
is away from and above the world and who
take things of life as their life supply (v. 13).

d. Insects that have wings and have legs above
their feet for leaping on the ground signify
persons who can live and move in a life that
is above the world and who can keep themselves from the world (vv. 21-22).

Day 4

D. We can eat Him by feasting on Him in the meetings on the unique ground of oneness:

1. The children of Israel could enjoy the produce
of the land in two ways: the common, private
way was to enjoy it as a common portion at
any time, in any place, and with anyone (Deut.
12:15); the special, corporate way was to enjoy
the top portion, the firstfruits and the firstlings, with all the Israelites at the appointed
feasts and in the unique place chosen by God
(vv. 5-7, 17-18).

2. Likewise, the enjoyment of Christ by the New
Testament believers is of two aspects: the
common, private aspect of enjoying Christ at
any time and at any place and the special, corporate aspect of enjoying the top portion of
Christ in the meetings of the proper church
life on the unique ground of oneness, the place
chosen by God (Col. 1:12; 1 Cor. 14:26).

Day 5

III. **The principle of the tree of life is the principle of dependence on God, and it is realized
throughout the whole Bible by those who lived
on the line of life:**

A. Abel contacted God in God's way (Gen. 4:4).

B. Seth and Enosh called upon the name of the Lord (v. 26).

C. Enoch walked with God (5:22-24).

D. Noah walked with God and worked together with God (6:8-9, 14).

E. Abraham lived in the appearing of God and called upon the name of the Lord (Acts 7:2; Gen. 12:7-8; 17:1; 18:1; James 2:23).

F. Moses lived in the appearing and the presence of God (Exo. 3:2, 16; 33:11, 13-15; 25:9).

G. The children of Israel journeyed in the presence of the Lord (13:21-22; Num. 14:14).

H. Joshua lived and worked in the presence of the Lord (Josh. 1:5-9).

I. Gideon fought in and with the presence of the Lord (Judg. 6:12, 16).

Day 6

J. Samuel prayed and called on the Lord (1 Sam. 12:23; 15:11; Psa. 99:6; Jer. 15:1).

K. David trusted in God, looked to God, and enjoyed God's life (1 Sam. 17:37, 45; 30:6; Psa. 27:4, 8, 14; 36:8-9).

L. Daniel prayed constantly and contacted the Lord continually in utter dependence on Him (Dan. 2:17-23; 6:10-11; 9:2-4; 10:1-3, 12).

M. The Lord Jesus as the tree of life and as the Son of God lived because of the Father (John 6:57; 14:10).

N. The New Testament believers live because of the Lord by eating Him and by abiding in Him so that He may abide in them (6:57; 15:5).

O. Paul lived out the Lord for His magnification (Gal. 2:20; Phil. 1:19-21a).

P. The church as the Body of Christ depends on Christ and lives by Christ as life (Eph. 1:22-23; Col. 3:4).

Q. The New Jerusalem is sustained by the river of water of life with the tree of life (Rev. 22:1-2, 14, 17).

Morning Nourishment

Gen. 2:9 And out of the ground Jehovah God caused to grow every tree that is pleasant to the sight and good for food, as well as the tree of life in the middle of the garden and the tree of the knowledge of good and evil.

John 1:4 In Him was life...

15:1 I am the true vine...

The first step of God's procedure in fulfilling His purpose was to create man as a vessel to contain Himself as life (Rom. 9:21, 23; 2 Cor. 4:7; 2 Tim. 2:21). (Gen. 2:7, footnote 2)

The second step of God's procedure in fulfilling His purpose was to place the created man in front of the tree of life, which signifies the Triune God embodied in Christ as life to man in the form of food. God's placing man in front of the tree of life indicates that God wanted man to receive Him as man's life by eating Him organically and assimilating Him metabolically, that God might become the very constituent of man's being. According to John 1:1 and 4, life is in the Word, who is God Himself. This life—the divine, eternal, uncreated life of God—is Christ (John 11:25; 14:6; Col. 3:4a), who is the embodiment of God (Col. 2:9). The tree of life grows along the two sides of the river of water of life (Rev. 22:1-2), indicating that it is a vine. Since Christ is a vine tree (John 15:1) and is also life, He is the tree of life. He was processed through incarnation, crucifixion, and resurrection that man might have life and live by eating Him (John 10:10b; 6:51, 57, 63). (Gen. 2:9, footnote 2)

Today's Reading

The tree of life causes man to be dependent on God (John 15:5), whereas the tree of knowledge causes man to rebel against God and to be independent from Him (cf. Gen. 3:5). The two trees issue in two lines—the line of life and the line of death—that run through the entire Bible and end in the book of Revelation. Death begins with the tree of knowledge (2:17) and ends with the lake of fire (Rev. 20:10, 14). Life begins with the tree of life and ends in the New

Jerusalem, the city of the water of life (22:1-2). (Gen. 2:9, footnote 3)
Genesis 2:9 says that the trees were good for food. Notice that the Bible does not say that the trees were good for producing materials, for the concept of Genesis is not that of human labor or achievement. Thus, no manufacturing materials are mentioned. The concept of Genesis 2 is fully focused on life. Thus, it says that the trees were good for food because food is related to life. Without food, we cannot live. Food maintains our life and satisfies us.

The tree of life was in the midst of the garden. If we study the record of Genesis 2, we will realize that, apart from the tree of knowledge of good and evil, no tree is mentioned by name except the tree of life. We do not know the names of the other trees, but we do know that there was a tree called the tree of life. This shows that the tree of life was the center.

This tree enables man to receive God as life. How can we prove this? The following books of the Bible reveal that God is life. Therefore, the tree of life in the garden was the indicator that God intends to be our life in the form of food. One day, according to the Gospel of John, God came in the flesh (John 1:1, 14). In Him was life (John 1:4). The life displayed by the tree of life in Genesis 2 was the life incarnated in Jesus, God in the flesh. Jesus told us that He Himself is life (John 14:6). Furthermore, John 15 tells us that Christ is a tree, the vine tree. On the one hand, He is a tree; on the other hand, He is life. When we put together all these portions from John, we see that Jesus is the tree of life. Jesus said that He is the bread of life, meaning that He has come to us as the tree of life in the form of food.

The tree of life typifies Christ who imparts life to man and who pleases and satisfies man (cf. John 15:1; Exo. 15:25). Christ imparts divine life into us, pleases us, and satisfies us. Many of us can testify of this. We can say, "Hallelujah! Jesus has imparted life to me. He satisfies me all the time." This is the tree of life. (*Life-study of Genesis*, pp. 139-141)

Further Reading: Life-study of Genesis, msg. 11

Enlightenment and inspiration: _____

_____

_____

_____

Morning Nourishment

Matt. But He answered and said, It is written, "Man shall
4:4 not live on bread alone, but on every word that proceeds out through the mouth of God."

John Jesus said to them, My food is to do the will of Him
4:34 who sent Me and to finish His work.

[handwritten: ...giving living water to the Samaritan woman]

God presented Himself to man in the form of food. This can be
clearly seen in the Gospel of John. John tells us that in the beginning was the Word, the Word was God, and in Him was life (1:1, 4).
One day He performed a miracle by feeding five thousand people
with five barley loaves and two fishes (6:9-13). Then the people
wanted to make Him a king. But He did not take that offer (v. 15).
He later told them that He came not to be a king to rule others
outwardly but to be the bread of life to be eaten (vv. 35, 57). He
came that we may eat Him. The Lord does not want us to consider
how to serve Him, how to worship Him, or how to glorify Him, but
He wants us to consider Him as our food. He came to present
Himself to us as life in the form of food. We have to take Him as
food by feeding on Him and eating Him. "He who eats Me, he also
shall live because of Me" (v. 57b). (*The Tree of Life,* pp. 9-10)

Today's Reading

We have to believe in the Lord Jesus because we need Him as
our life (John 3:16, 36). To believe in Him is to receive Him into us
as life (1:12-13). He is not only our objective Savior but also our
subjective life. We need such a life. After receiving Him, the problem with us is not related to work, to service, or to worship, but to
eating. How do you eat, what do you eat, and how much do you
eat? Immediately after the creation of man, God put man in front
of the tree of life that man may take the tree of life as his food. This
simply means that God presented Himself to man as life in the
form of food. God had no intention to ask man to do things for
Him. God's intention is that man would simply take God Himself
as his food, that man would feed on God.

I hope that the Lord would change your concept from doing to
eating. If you would become not merely a doing Christian but an

eating Christian, that would be wonderful. In today's Christianity the emphasis is on doing and working. Christianity has been degraded into a doing religion, a working religion, a toiling religion. But God's first intention is not to have man toiling, but to have man feasting and feeding on Him, to have man enjoying God Himself. John 4:24 tells us that we must worship God, but we must ask what the word "worship" means. According to the full context of John 4, the Lord's meaning is that to drink of Him as the living water in verse 14 is to worship Him in verse 24. When you drink of Him as the living water, that means that you worship Him. The more you drink of Him, the more you will be filled with Him and the more He will be worshipped by you. The best way to worship the Lord is to drink of Him, to feed on Him, to enjoy Him, to take Him in.

The Lord's intention is to present Himself as food to us day by day. In the Gospel of John, the Lord is first seen as life (1:4), as the bread of life (6:35), as the water of life (4:14), and as the breath of life, the air (20:22). He is life, food, drink, and air. All this is not for you to be a doing Christian but to be an enjoying Christian. You have to enjoy the Lord as life, as food, as water, and as air. You have to breathe Him in, to drink of Him, and to feed on Him in order to live by Him and in Him.

We also have to learn how to enjoy Him. He is life, food, water, and air to us, but how can we enjoy Him? If we are going to enjoy the Lord, we have to open ourselves, not superficially but in a deep way. We should not only open our mind, or even our heart, but we also have to open our spirit.

If you would open yourself to the Lord in such a way, you will see how real, available, and precious the Lord is. You will sense His presence within, and you will be filled with Him. He is not only the life to you, but He is also the food (the bread of life), the drink (the water of life), and the air (the breath of life) to you. All these things are related to the Lord as the tree of life. (*The Tree of Life*, pp. 10-12, 14)

Further Reading: The Tree of Life, chs. 1-2

Enlightenment and inspiration: _____

_____

_____

_____

Morning Nourishment

Acts And he beheld...a certain vessel...in which were all
10:11-15 the four-footed animals and reptiles of the earth and
birds of heaven. And a voice came to him: Rise up,
Peter; slay and eat! But Peter said, By no means, Lord,
for I have never eaten anything common and unclean.
And a voice *came* to him again a second time: The
things that God has cleansed, do not make common.

Discernment in diet is a matter of discernment...in what we
eat....Why...must we take care of our eating if we are to live a
holy life?...Leviticus is a book of types...which bear a particular
significance....All [the animals mentioned in Leviticus 11] typify
persons; they are figures that describe different kinds of persons.
This is proved by Acts 10:9b-14, 27-29. Peter "beheld heaven
opened, and a certain vessel like a great sheet descending, being
let down by four corners onto the earth, in which were all the four-
footed animals and reptiles of the earth and birds of heaven"
(vv. 11-12). At first, Peter did not understand that these animals,
reptiles, and birds were figures of people. Eventually he came to
understand this, for in the house of Cornelius there were people,
not beasts (vv. 27-28). (*Life-study of Leviticus,* p. 313)

Today's Reading

When we eat we contact something that is outside of us, something that has nothing to do with us. However, if we eat that thing,
it can affect us inside. In Leviticus 11 the things we eat signify
people, and eating signifies our contacting of people....Whatever
we contact we will receive, and whatever we receive will reconsti-
tute us, making us a different kind of person from what we are now.

In [Leviticus 11] five categories of animals are covered: first,
the beasts, including cattle; second, the aquatic animals...; third, the
birds...; fourth, the insects; and finally, the creeping things. All
creeping things are unclean, but in the other four categories some
animals are clean and others are unclean.

Animals that divide the hoof and chew the cud (vv. 2-3) signify
persons who have discernment in their activities and who receive

the word of God with much reconsideration....We need to discern not only what is good and what is bad but also what is of our spirit and what is of our flesh, as well as what things are of the new man and what things are of the old man.

Aquatic animals having fins and scales (v. 9) signify persons who can move and act freely in the world and at the same time resist its influence. Fins help fish to move, to act, in water according to their wishes. Because they have fins, fish may even swim against the current.

Scales protect the fish and keep those fish which live in salt water from being salted. Fish may live in salt water for years without being salted because they have scales to keep the salt away. Therefore, fins strengthen the fish to move, and scales protect them from being salted.

Birds that have wings for flying and that eat seeds of life as the food supply (cf. vv. 13-19) signify persons who can live and move in a life that is away from and above the world and who take things of life as their supply of life....[Clean birds] are able to fly away from and above the world...[and] eat seeds of life as their food supply. On the contrary, the unclean birds in 11:13-19 do not feed on seeds. Because the seeds of life do not satisfy them, these unclean birds feed on carcasses....For this reason, we must be careful in contacting those who feed on the things of death.

Insects having wings and having jointed legs above their feet for leaping on the ground (vv. 21-22) signify persons who can live and move in a life that is above the world and who can keep themselves from the world.

If we intend to live in a holy way, we need to exercise care concerning our contact with people. Contacting people is a very important matter, especially for us Christians. We should not contact others without caution, and we should not form friendships in a careless way. Careless friendships, the Bible indicates, will corrupt us. (*Life-study of Leviticus*, pp. 313-317, 319)

Further Reading: Life-study of Leviticus, msg. 36

Enlightenment and inspiration: _____

_____

_____

_____

Morning Nourishment

Deut. You may not eat within your gates the tithe of your
12:17-18 grain or of your new wine or of your fresh oil, nor the
firstborn of your herd or of your flock, or any of your
vows which you vow or of your freewill offerings or of
the heave offering of your hand; but you shall eat
them before Jehovah your God in the place which
Jehovah your God will choose...

The children of Israel could enjoy the rich produce of the good land in two ways. The common, private way was to enjoy it as a common portion at any time, in any place, and with anyone (Deut. 12:15). The special, corporate way was to enjoy the top portion, the firstfruits and the firstlings, with all the Israelites at the appointed feasts and in the unique place chosen by God (see footnote 1 on v. 5). Likewise, the enjoyment of Christ by the New Testament believers is of two aspects—the common, private aspect of enjoying Christ at any time and at any place, and the special, corporate aspect of enjoying the top portion of Christ in the meetings of the proper church life on the unique ground of oneness, the place chosen by God. (Deut. 12:17, footnote 1)

Today's Reading

The principle of the tree of life and the principle of the tree of knowledge of good and evil are realized throughout the whole Bible. All the negative things in the Bible are on the line of the tree of knowledge, and all the positive things are on the line of the tree of life....These two lines...[can] carry us through the entire Scripture.

Firstly, man was induced to eat of the tree of knowledge. As a result, man fell. The descendants of fallen man did not depend upon God at all. They relied upon their knowledge. According to Genesis 4, the first human culture was invented, and this culture developed until it became the corrupted world of Noah. During the time of Noah, God judged the earth by the flood. Noah's descendants became another race, but this race still did not depend upon God. Eventually, the second human culture...erected the tower and city of Babel. Then God called Abraham out of that fallen race. By this we can see the development of the two lines. Strictly speaking, the line of life began with Adam, who was fallen and redeemed, and continued through Abel, Enoch, Noah, Abraham, Isaac, Jacob, and so many Israelites. On this line of life we have the tent of Noah, the tent of Abraham, the tabernacle, and the temple. The line of knowledge began with Cain and continued through all the ungodly people. On the line of knowledge we have the city of Enoch, Babel, Sodom, the treasure cities of Pharaoh, and Babylon, which captured the things on the line of life.

We find the same two lines in the New Testament. Although the Old Testament and the law were originally on the line of life, the Jewish religionists treated them as mere knowledge and put them on the line of knowledge. The Pharisees used the Old Testament in the way of knowledge. When the Lord Jesus came, the religious leaders were altogether on the line of knowledge. Only the Lord Jesus Himself was on the line of life. Then He brought His disciples to the line of life. On the day of Pentecost, His disciples put many other people on the line of life. Thus, at that time, there was the Jewish religion on the line of knowledge and the church on the line of life. However, not long afterward, the church was degraded, falling from the living Christ to dead scriptural knowledge, and became Christianity. The church was on the line of life, but Christianity was on the line of knowledge. Revelation 17 tells us that eventually Christianity will become the great, religious Babylon, and Revelation 18 says that the world system will result in the great political Babylon....The great Babylon is the culmination of the line of knowledge. The overcomers among the Christians through all the centuries never have shifted from the line of life to the line of knowledge. They will remain on the line of life until the end when it ultimately issues in the New Jerusalem.

Life is God Himself,...[and] the principle of life is to be dependent on God for everything. If you depend on God, everything is life. (*Life-study of Genesis*, pp. 172-173, 177)

Further Reading: Life-study of Genesis, msg. 14

Enlightenment and inspiration: _____

_____

_____

_____

Morning Nourishment

Gen. And Enoch walked with God, and he was not, for God
5:24 took him.
12:7-8 ...And there [Abram] built an altar to Jehovah who
had appeared to him. And he proceeded from there to
the mountain on the east of Bethel...and...he built an
altar to Jehovah and called upon the name of Jehovah.

Throughout the Bible we have two lines—the line of the tree of
life and the line of the tree of knowledge.

Apparently the tree of life has been closed to man [since Genesis 3]; actually through the promised redemption it has been available throughout the ages for God's people to touch, enjoy, and
experience. Now...I want to give you many of the positive persons
on this line of life....We begin with Abel.

The characteristic of Abel's life was that he contacted God in
God's way (Gen. 4:4). Do not say that as long as you contact God
everything is all right. In whose way do you contact God—in your
way or God's?...The source [of man's own way of contacting God]
is man's troublesome mind, which can produce nothing except
knowledge. Hence, men contact God in the way of knowledge, not
in the way of life. Abel, however, contacted God in His way [Gen.
4:4]....Cain contacted God in his own way. God's way is life; Cain's
way is knowledge. (*Life-study of Genesis*, pp. 181, 183-184)

Today's Reading

After Abel was slain,...Seth and Enosh were raised up to continue [the line of life]. These two generations had one outstanding
characteristic—they began to call upon the name of the Lord (Gen.
4:26). They not only prayed, but called on the name of the Lord.

The characteristic of Enoch's life was that he walked with God
(Gen. 5:22, 24). We are not told that he worked for God or that he
did great things for God, but that he walked with God. This is very
meaningful....The fact that Enoch walked with God proves that
he loved God. He simply loved to be in the presence of God.

Noah followed Enoch's footsteps and also walked with God (Gen.
6:9)....As Noah walked with God, God showed him a vision of what

He wanted to do in that age. Noah received the vision of the ark.
…Like Noah, we should not act according to our concept. Whatever we do and work should be according to the vision we received
in walking with the Lord.

Abraham was transfused with the appearing of the God of
glory. While Abraham was in Ur of the Chaldees, the God of glory
appeared to him and attracted him (Acts 7:2). According to the
record in Genesis, God appeared to Abraham several other times
as well (Gen. 12:7; 17:1; 18:1). Abraham was not a giant of faith by
himself; he was as weak as we are. The God of glory appeared to
Abraham again and again, each time transfusing and infusing
His divine elements into him, enabling him to live by the faith of
God.…In addition to experiencing the appearings of God, Abraham called upon the name of the Lord (Gen. 12:7-8).

One day, in the midst of his disappointment, God came [and]…
appeared to Moses in a vision of a burning bush, a bush that
burned without being consumed (Exo. 3:2, 16). Moses was sur-
prised and turned aside to see this bush. It was as if God was saying to Moses, "Moses, you must be like this burning bush. Do not
burn by yourself or act by yourself. You had a good heart, but you
acted in the wrong way."…Moses learned to cease from his own
knowledge, his own way, his own energy, and his own activities.
Moses began to live, as his grandfathers had done, in the presence
and the appearing of the Lord. No longer did he act out of himself.
From that time onward, he was one with God.

For a period of forty years the children of Israel journeyed in
the presence of the Lord (Exo. 13:21-22; Num. 14:14). They had
the pillar of cloud by day and the pillar of fire by night. The Israelites did not journey according to their opinion, but simply followed the movement of the pillar.…They also ate manna, the
heavenly food, day after day, meaning they enjoyed God as the
tree of life. Thus, even in the wilderness we see the line of the tree
of life. (*Life-study of Genesis,* pp. 184-187, 189-191)

Further Reading: Life-study of Genesis, msg. 13

Enlightenment and inspiration: _____

good Egypt edmeah
sing in speech
that could lead to tree of knowledge
(but couldn't bring him to anywhere
→ escape   to wilderness. & get old —

Morning Nourishment

John **As the living Father has sent Me and I live because of**
6:57-58 **the Father, so he who eats Me, he also shall live**
  because of Me. This is the bread which came down
  out of heaven, not as the fathers ate and died; he who
  eats this bread shall live forever.

Samuel was another wonderful person in the Old Testament, a
man who prayed for the children of God continually. The Bible says
that Samuel told the people that he would not sin against the Lord
in ceasing to pray for them (1 Sam. 12:23)....The Bible refers to
Samuel as a man who called upon the name of the Lord (Psa. 99:6)
and as a man who stood in the presence of God (Jer. 15:1)....By
standing in the presence of the Lord and by calling on the name of
the Lord, he enjoyed the Lord, partaking of Him as the tree of life.

David was a man who trusted in God and looked to Him (1 Sam.
17:37, 45; 30:6). The secret of David's life was that he desired to
dwell continually in the house of God and to behold His beauty
(Psa. 27:4, 8, 14). This means that he enjoyed the presence of God.
Moreover, he enjoyed God as the fatness and as the river of joy
(Psa. 36:8-9). David said, "With You is the fountain of life." This
proves that even in ancient times David enjoyed God's life as the
tree of life and as the river flowing within him. (*Life-study of Genesis*, pp. 192-193)

Today's Reading

[Daniel was] a man who prayed constantly and contacted the
Lord continually (Dan. 6:10-11; 9:3-4; 10:2-3, 12)....Daniel's prayer
life issued out of a holy life. He lived a holy life in the heathen land
of Babylon. For example, Daniel refused to eat the king's food, the
food which was first offered to idols and then used to feed the king
and his people (Dan. 1:8). Daniel refused that food, and he enjoyed
God very much. He enjoyed God as the tree of life.

The first person on the line of life in the New Testament was
the Lord Jesus. Jesus not only enjoyed the tree of life; He was the
tree of life. He Himself said that He came from the Father and
that He lived by the Father (John 6:57). He did not live according

to knowledge and learning. He lived, walked, and worked according to the Father who was working within Him (John 14:10).

Our destiny as New Testament believers is simply to abide in the Lord and to allow the Lord to abide in us (John 15:5). This means that we enjoy the Lord. The Lord Jesus told us that we must eat Him, for he who eats Him shall live because of Him (John 6:57; 14:19). We must eat the Lord Jesus because He is our bread of life, our tree of life. The tree of life is life presented in the form of food. In John 6 the Lord presented Himself as the life supply also in the form of food, telling us that He is the bread of life (v. 35) and that His flesh is eatable (v. 55). If we eat Him, we will have Him as our life and as the life supply by which we live. This is the genuine enjoyment of the tree of life.

Paul was an example of a man who lived out the Lord. In Galatians 2:20 Paul said that Christ lived in him and that the life which he lived he lived by the faith of the Lord Jesus. Paul was saying that he himself had been crucified and buried, and that it was Christ who lived in him. Eventually Paul could say, "For to me, to live is Christ" (Phil. 1:21). Christ was his life and his life supply, for Paul enjoyed Christ as the tree of life.

The church is the Body of Christ. It is impossible for the body not to enjoy the head. The body cannot be separated from the head, for such separation means death. The entire church is the Body of Christ, depending on Christ and living by Christ as life (Eph. 1:23; Col. 3:4). By this we can see that the church may enjoy Christ as the tree of life.

At the end of the Bible we see the consummation of the tree of life—the New Jerusalem. In the center of this city we see the river of life, which proceeds out of the throne of God and the Lamb, and in which grows the tree of life that bears fruit every month (Rev. 22:1-2). Our destiny and our portion for eternity will be the enjoyment of the tree of life and the water of life….This is the consummation of the line of life. (*Life-study of Genesis,* pp. 193-195)

Further Reading: Life-study of Genesis, msg. 15

Enlightenment and inspiration: _____

_____

_____

_____

509

1145   1151   1331   12

1148

Hymns, #1143

1   The tree of life, how sweet the fruit,
    With God as life complete.
    I once was dead, but now I live,
    Was starved, but now I eat.

2   'Twas God that brought me to the tree,
    With Christ Himself as meat;
    How precious did that tree become
    When I began to eat.

3   The Lord Himself is food to me,
    He is my life supply;
    He will my pure enjoyment be,
    None else can satisfy.

4   I freely eat this living tree,
    For eating is the way
    To put God's life inside of me,
    To live by Him today.

Composition for prophecy with main point and sub-points: _____

The Church as the Body of Christ—
the Mysterious Organism
in God's New Testament Economy

Scripture Reading: Eph. 1:22-23; 4:4-6, 11-16, 22-24, 30;
5:25b-27, 29; Rom. 8:2-13; 12:4-8

Day 1

I. **The great turning wheel of God's economy has the Body of Christ as its axis:**
   A. The move of God's New Testament economy is like the turning of a great wheel (cf. Ezek. 1:15-21).
   B. This turning wheel in God's economy has the Body of Christ as its axis:
      1. All of God's move and work today are joined to and for the Body of Christ (Eph. 1:22-23).
      2. The New Jerusalem as the ultimate consummation of God's work is the axis of God's move in the whole universe (Rev. 21:2, 11; 22:1).

Day 2

II. **The Body of Christ as the axis of God's economy is the organism of the Triune God:**
   A. The church is not an organization manufactured by man but an organism produced by the Triune God as life.
   B. The true vine, a portrait of Christ, is an organism by which the Triune God accomplishes His eternal economy (John 15:1):
      1. A tree with life is organic and is able to produce fruit.
      2. A wooden table without life is organizational and is unable to produce fruit.

Day 3

   C. This divine organism is the structure of the union and mingling of all the believers with the Triune God (Eph. 4:4-6):
      1. The Father is the person who is over all (managing and caring), through all (penetrating and joining), and in all (dwelling and living) (v. 6).
      2. The Son is the element of life; through believing, the believers are joined to the element of Christ's new life, and through baptism, they

are cut off from the element of the old adamic life (v. 5).

3. The Spirit is the essence of life; the Spirit of the life of Christ is the essence of the Body of Christ, and the hope is the saturation of the Body of Christ with the splendor of this essence so that the Body of Christ may enter into the glory of the life of Christ (v. 4; Col. 1:27).

D. The metamorphic change of this divine organism is the mingling of God and man (Eph. 4:22-24):

1. This metamorphic change is the putting off of the old man, which is being corrupted according to lust, and the putting on of the new man, which was created according to God (vv. 22, 24).

2. This metamorphic change is accomplished through the renewing of the believers in the spirit of their mind (v. 23).

3. This metamorphic change is accomplished through the redemption by the saturating of the Holy Spirit of God as the seal (v. 30).

4. This metamorphic change is accomplished through the nourishing, sanctifying, and washing of Christ's word of life (5:25b-27, 29):

   a. Nourishing affords the supply in life and provides at the same time the warm, tender, and loving cherishing.

   b. To be sanctified is to be separated unto and saturated with God and thus to be transformed (v. 26a).

   c. Washing removes the spots and wrinkles in order that the divine organism may become holy and glorious.

Day 4

Korean

E. The growth of this divine organism and the organic building up of the organism by itself are in the divine life (4:11-16):

1. The gifted ones in this divine organism perfect others to be like them to do the work of the ministry for the organic building up of the Body of Christ (vv. 11-12).

2. The growth of this divine organism in the divine life equals the organic building up of the organism by itself in the divine life (vv. 13b-16):

   a. We need to hold to truth in love and grow up into the Head, Christ, in all things (vv. 13b, 15).

   b. Out from the Head, all the Body, being joined together through every joint of the rich supply and being knit together through the operation in the measure of each one part, grows gradually unto the organic building up of itself in love (v. 16).

Day 5

F. The living of this divine organism is the corporate and organic living of the Body of Christ (Rom. 12:5):

   1. All the members live together by taking Christ as life (Col. 3:3-4a).

   2. All the members care for one another (1 Cor. 12:25-27).

   3. This living is an organic living produced by the union and mingling of the Triune God with the tripartite man (Rom. 8:2-13):

      a. The law of the Spirit of life is the key to the mysterious organism in God's New Testament economy; we can cooperate with this law by prayer and by having a spirit of dependence (v. 2; 1 Thes. 5:17).

      b. Through the law of the Spirit of life, we were first enlivened in our spirit by the Spirit of Christ (Rom. 8:2, 9-10).

      c. Next, we are enlivened in the mind of our soul by the spreading Spirit of God (v. 6b).

      d. Lastly, we are enlivened in our mortal body by the indwelling Spirit of God (v. 11).

      e. For this reason, we have to set our mind on the spirit, walk according to the spirit, and put to death the practices of the body through the indwelling Spirit of God (vv. 6b, 4b, 11, 13).

Day 6

G. The service of this divine organism is the corporate organic service of the Body of Christ (12:4-8):

   1. Every member is necessary (1 Cor. 12:14-22).

2. Every member functions organically according to the operation in the measure of each one part.

3. This service is the organic service of the New Testament priesthood of the gospel (1 Pet. 2:5, 9):

   a. We need to preach the gospel to save sinners and offer them as sacrifices to God (Rom. 15:16).

   b. We need to nourish the believers and help them to grow so that they can offer themselves as living sacrifices to God (John 21:15; 1 Pet. 2:2; Rom. 12:1).

   c. We need to perfect the saints so that they may do the work of the ministry unto the organic building up of the Body of Christ (Eph. 4:11-16).

   d. We need to lead the saints to prophesy, to speak for God, for the organic building up of the church (1 Cor. 14:1, 3-5, 12, 24, 31).

   e. We need to labor and struggle in all wisdom to present to God every saint full-grown in Christ (Col. 1:28-29).

Morning Nourishment

Ezek. And as I watched the living creatures, I saw a wheel
1:15 upon the earth beside the living creatures, for *each of*
      their four faces.
Eph. And He subjected all things under His feet and gave
1:22-23 Him *to be* Head over all things to the church, which is
      His Body, the fullness of the One who fills all in all.

[In Ezekiel 1] we have four wheels turning....The move of God's
New Testament economy is like the turning of a big wheel (cf. Ezek.
1:15-21). Today...everywhere people are talking about democ-
racy. This is indeed a great change. When we come back to the
Bible, we first see at the beginning of Revelation the scene at the
throne in heaven. Following that we see the move on the earth,
represented by the four horses (Rev. 6:1-8 with footnotes). The
first horse is the white horse, which, together with its rider, sym-
bolizes the spreading of the gospel. It takes the lead in the entire
move on earth. When we look at the world situation, especially at
the changes in eastern Europe, we know that this is the turn of
the great wheel of the age. But we have to remember that we are
in a bigger and greater wheel, which is the move of God's New
Testament economy.

We know that every wheel has an axis; it is the center of the
wheel. The great turning wheel of God's economy has the Body of
Christ as the axis and the center. In a certain sense according to
the truth, we can say that this axis is Christ. But as far as God's
New Testament economy is concerned, this axis is the church, the
Body of Christ. This is why we say here that the turning wheel of
God's economy has the Body of Christ as its axis. This means that
all of God's move and work today are joined to the church and are
for the church, the Body of Christ (Eph. 1:22). (*The Mysteries in
God's New Testament Economy,* pp. 62-63)

Today's Reading

If we know something about world history and would spend
some time to study the Old Testament prophecies, we have to bow
down and worship the Lord that indeed everything in the universe

and all the world situations, whether political, military, industrial, commercial, scientific, or educational, have the Body of Christ as the center. They are all joined to and are for the Body of Christ.

We moved to Taiwan from the mainland in the second half of 1949. The world situation was tense. We decided to forget about everything and seize the opportunity to spread the gospel. First, we printed big quantities of gospel tracts in proportion to the population of Taipei. We divided up the city into districts according to the streets and passed out these tracts from house to house. Second, we made huge gospel posters and posted them at train stations, crossroads, and other important places. We even posted them by the doors of the brothers' and sisters' homes. Third, we sent out gospel teams to promote a gospel atmosphere along the large and small streets. In addition, every week, we went to the New Park to preach the gospel. We did this for four or five years, and our number increased from three or five hundred to forty or fifty thousand. None of us was affected by the world situation. From that time until now, after so many seasons of battering storms and rain, Taiwan is still solid as a rock. It has even made such miraculous achievements in recent years. I believe all these happenings are for the move of God's gospel. We know that the entire world situation is for the Body of Christ.

Furthermore, the New Jerusalem, as the ultimate consummation of God's work, is the axis of God's move in the whole universe (Rev. 21:2, 11; 22:1). The whole universe is full of God's move, and the ultimate achievement of this entire move is the New Jerusalem. The church today is the miniature of the New Jerusalem in the future, and the Lord's recovery on earth represents His church. This is why I have a strong burden during this conference to fellowship with all of you again concerning the church as the mysterious organism in God's New Testament economy. (*The Mysteries in God's New Testament Economy*, pp. 63-64)

Further Reading: The Mysteries in God's New Testament Economy,
   "A Foreword to the Conference"

Enlightenment and inspiration: _____

_____

_____

_____

Morning Nourishment

Eph. One Body and one Spirit, even as also you were called
4:4-6 in one hope of your calling; one Lord, one faith, one
baptism; one God and Father of all, who is over all
and through all and in all.
John I am the true vine, and My Father is the husbandman.
15:1

The Body of Christ as the axis of God's economy is the orga-
nism of the Triune God. This is not a small thing. According to
Ephesians 4:4-6, we can say strongly that the Triune God is in the
Body of Christ today. Here it mentions one Body, one Spirit, one
Lord, and one God, who is over all, through all, and in us all.
According to the human understanding, the Triune God is in
heaven. But according to the revelation of the Bible,...the Triune
God is in the Body....It is true that the Triune God is in heaven,
but mainly...He is working in the Body of Christ. Today, the Triune God is doing only one central work, which is the building up of
the Body of Christ. Everything that God is doing in the universe is
for this central work....If we truly see this revelation, our life and
service will be absolutely different. (*The Mysteries in God's New
Testament Economy*, p. 64)

Today's Reading

Everything works together and coordinates together for the
Body of Christ. This Body is not a humanly manufactured organization but an organism produced by the Triune God as life. Hence,
the church as the Body of Christ is not a congregation but a Body. It
is not a human organization, but the organism of the Triune God.

[A] wooden table is a dead organization. It cannot move. I am a
living organism and am very lively. Every part of me is functioning. The old system in Christianity has annulled all the organic
functions of the Christians....They cannot function anymore and
are like those without any spiritual life. What is left is just a clergy-
laity system. In the Lord's recovery, we have to overturn this so
that every believer may become alive and may function for the
organic Body to be expressed.

The spiritual life which is in every saved person has its capacities that come with its nature. According to its capacity, it likes to move, to function, and to serve the Lord. Apparently, the meetings with one speaking and all listening appeal to the Christian taste. But actually, the capacity within a Christian's nature has no taste for that. Everyone who knows this…is for the mutual speaking and mutual listening, because the mutual speaking and mutual listening match the capacity of our spiritual life.

Our human body is a living organism. That is why it has to be active. The less the body moves, the easier it is for it to become sick. The more it moves, the healthier it becomes. In the practice of the new way during the past five years, our study gave us a conclusion in four steps: 1) the preaching of the gospel for the saving of sinners, 2) the nourishing of the new ones in their homes, 3) the setting up of the group meetings for the mutual perfecting, and 4) the prophesying in the Lord's Day meeting by everyone for the release of the riches of Christ and the supply to the members, with the result that the Body of Christ is built up. These four steps are…scriptural and fully match the capacity in our spiritual life. Because of this, we must promote this matter today so that all the brothers and sisters…can develop the capacity of their spiritual life and can become living and functioning members.

The true vine in John 15…is the organism in the eternal economy of the Triune God. The Lord Jesus is the tree. We are the branches. When we are joined to and mingled with Him, we become the organism of the Triune God. The Triune God is operating and working in this true vine today. Hence, we should not despise ourselves, for we are the Body of Christ. We have a part in the true vine that the Triune God is cultivating.…The Lord's recovery is carrying out the mingling of the Triune God with this organism so that He can live, operate, and work here for the wheel of His economy to be turned. (*The Mysteries in God's New Testament Economy,* pp. 65-66)

Further Reading: The Mysteries in God's New Testament Economy, ch. 3

Enlightenment and inspiration: _____

_____

_____

_____

Morning Nourishment

Eph. That you put off...the old man...and *that* you be
4:22-24 renewed in the spirit of your mind and put on the
new man, which was created according to God in
righteousness and holiness of the reality.

5:25-27 Husbands, love your wives even as Christ also loved
the church and gave Himself up for her that He
might sanctify her, cleansing *her* by the washing
of the water in the word, that He might present
the church to Himself glorious, not having spot or
wrinkle or any such things, but that she would be
holy and without blemish.

This organism is the structure of the union and mingling of
all the believers with the Triune God (Eph. 4:4-6). This is truly
a tremendous thing. We who have believed in Him are now
able to be joined to and mingled with Him. In this structure of
union and mingling, God the Father is the person. He is over
all, managing and caring for all, and is through all, penetrat-
ing and joining all, and is even in us all, dwelling and living in
all. In addition, God the Son is here as the element and factor
of life. Through baptism, we the believers have been cut off
from the element of the old Adamic life, and through believing, we have been joined to the element of Christ's new life.
Moreover, we have God the Spirit as the essence of life. The
Spirit of the life of Christ is the essence of the Body of Christ.
The hope is the saturation of the Body of Christ with the
splendor of this essence that the Body of Christ may enter into
the glory of the life of Christ (Col. 1:27). Now we are all in the
organism of the Triune God. This Christ who is the Spirit of
life is saturating us continually with His essence until we
express the splendor of this essence, which is the redemption
of our bodies into glory. (*The Mysteries in God's New Testament
Economy*, p. 67)

Today's Reading

Following this, let us consider the metamorphic change of

this organism—the mingling of God and man (Eph. 4:22-24). Although the Body of Christ has been cut off from the old creation, the "skin" of the old creation has not been fully shed. There is still the need for the metamorphic change, which is the putting off of the old man that has been corrupted by lust and the putting on of the new man that is created according to God in righteousness and holiness of the truth. Hence, every day we are putting off the old man and putting on the new man. The more we put off the old man, the more we will put on the new man. This metamorphic change is accomplished through the renewing in the spirit of the mind of the believers. When the Spirit of God continually saturates our minds, we have the spirit of our mind. It is in this spirit that we are renewed and are transformed.

This metamorphic change of the organism, the mingling of God and man, is also accomplished through the redemption by the saturating of the Holy Spirit of God as the seal (Eph. 4:30). The more the Holy Spirit saturates us, the more our bodies are redeemed. The parts of our being that have not been saturated by this seal are not yet redeemed. The Holy Spirit is in us as the seal. From the day that we were saved, God has been sealing us with His element for the purpose of saturating our whole being until our bodies are fully transformed and redeemed. This kind of metamorphic change is also through the nourishing, sanctifying, and washing of Christ's word of life (Eph. 5:25b-27, 29). In the Lord's word, there is not only the washing water, but also the nourishing element and the sanctifying power. The nourishing affords the supply in life and provides the warm, tender, loving cherishing. Sanctification separates us unto God and transforms us. The washing removes the spots and wrinkles so that the divine organism may become holy and glorious. (*The Mysteries in God's New Testament Economy,* pp. 67-68)

Further Reading: A Thorough View of the Body of Christ, ch. 2

Enlightenment and inspiration: _____

_____

_____

_____

Morning Nourishment

Eph. **And He Himself gave some...for the perfecting of the**
4:11-12 **saints unto the work of the ministry, unto the building**
up of the Body of Christ.
15-16 **...Holding to truth in love, we may grow up into Him in**
all things, who is the Head, Christ, out from whom all
the Body, being joined together and being knit together
through every joint of the rich supply and *through* the
operation in the measure of each one part, causes the
growth of the Body unto the building up of itself in love.

Let us consider the growth of this divine organism and the organic building up of the organism by itself (Eph. 4:11-16). The gifted ones in this organism perfect others so that they can also become gifted ones and can do the work of the ministry for the organic building up of the Body of Christ. Furthermore, the growth of this organism in the divine life equals the organic building up of the organism by itself in the divine life. When a baby is born, he needs to grow by drinking milk. This growth is the building, and both the growth and the building are organic functions. To build a house is organizational; it is not organic. It is done by putting together different materials. It is an organizational building. But our body is not like this. Our body is built up organically. It is not built up by adding some flesh or skin from without, but by the growth of itself through eating. (*The Mysteries in God's New Testament Economy*, pp. 68-69)

Today's Reading

The most difficult lesson to learn for us who are working for the Lord is to not have an organizational work but to have an organic work. Many times our nourishing and perfecting of others are merely organizational methods. We only add something onto others. We should learn of Paul, who helped others to grow in life. In 1 Corinthians 3:6 he said, "I planted, Apollos watered, but God caused the growth." If we want to have an organic work, we need to have this kind of realization and attitude. We should not depend on our own methods. We are only those who plant and water. We can only do our part to nourish others, to fellowship and pray with others, and to supply them with some words of life. In the depth of our being, we still look to the God who gives life to work in man. In this way, we are not adding something to man, but are supplying others from within so that they can grow in life and be built up.

When we lead and help others, we have to point out a way for them to learn to practice holding to truth in love and to grow up in all things into the Head, Christ. By this, they will be able to touch and enjoy Christ, and Christ will have the preeminent place in them. They will then grow and be built up. In this way, out from the Head, all the Body, being joined together through every joint of the rich supply and being knit together through the operation in the measure of each one part, will be able to grow gradually unto the organic building up of itself in love. Hence, strictly speaking, it is not we who are building. We are only affording others a little supply, through which they grow and are built up organically. (*The Mysteries in God's New Testament Economy*, p. 69)

At birth, an infant is perfect organically; that is, the infant has all the necessary organs. However, a child is not functionally perfect at birth. Organically, a mother cannot help her child, for she cannot add any organs to the child. But she can help him functionally by feeding him so that he will grow normally....This principle also applies to the church as the new man. In Ephesians 2:15 we see the creation of the new man organically, but in 4:13-16 we see the perfecting of the new man in relation to his function.

Our growth in life is to grow into the Head, Christ, but our function in the Body is to function out from Him. The phrase "each one part" refers to every member of the Body. Every member of the Body of Christ has its own measure which works for the growth of the Body. The Body causes the growth of itself through the supplying joints and working parts. The growth of the Body is the increase of Christ in the church, which results in the building up of the Body itself. (*Life-study of Ephesians*, p. 768)

Further Reading: Life-study of Ephesians, msgs. 80, 92

Enlightenment and inspiration: _____

_____

_____

_____

Morning Nourishment

Rom. So we who are many are one Body in Christ, and indi-
12:5 vidually members one of another.
 8:2 For the law of the Spirit of life has freed me in Christ
      Jesus from the law of sin and of death.
Col. For you died, and your life is hidden with Christ in
3:3-4 God. When Christ our life is manifested, then you also
      will be manifested with Him in glory.

Finally, let us look at the living and service of this organism.
The living of this organism is the corporate and organic living of
the Body of Christ (Rom. 12:5). All the members live together by
taking Christ as life (Col. 3:3-4a), and all care for one another
(1 Cor. 12:25-27). This kind of living is also an organic living produced by the union and mingling of the Triune God with the tripartite man (Rom. 8:2-13). We are men of three parts. Through
the law of the Spirit of life, we were first enlivened in our spirit
by the Spirit of Christ. Next, we are enlivened in the mind of our
soul by the spreading Spirit of God. Lastly, we are enlivened in
our mortal body by the indwelling Spirit of God....For this reason, we have to set our mind on the spirit, walk according to the
spirit, and put to death the practices of the body through the
indwelling Spirit of God. This is the living of the tripartite man
mingled with the Triune God. He is the Dweller, and we are His
dwelling. He and we are mingled as one. We live together to
become the organic Body of Christ. (*The Mysteries in God's New
Testament Economy*, p. 70)

Today's Reading

The law of the Spirit of life is the key to the mysterious organism in God's New Testament economy. The mysterious organism
in God's New Testament economy is a matter of Christ being our
life (Col. 3:4a). With life, there is the law. Without the law of life,
what we have is just outward regulations and ordinances.

In the whole universe, the highest and greatest law is one in
which the Triune God is the law, because the Triune God is the
highest, richest, and best life. There is no other life that is higher

and better than the Triune God. Hence, there is no other law that is higher and better than the Triune God as law....What Romans 8:2-13 talks about is actually this law. Verse 2 tells us in plain words that the law of the Spirit of life has freed us. After this it talks about the processed Triune God working Himself into us, the tripartite man. First, He enters into our spirit to make our spirit life (v. 10). Next, He saturates our mind, so that our mind also becomes life (v. 6). Finally, He permeates our bodies from the soul to which our mind belongs, giving life to our mortal bodies (v. 11). The purpose of the Triune God dispensing Himself into our whole being in this way is not merely to be life but to be a law.

God the Father is the source of life in the Body of Christ. This results in God the Son being the life element of the Body of Christ, and as the element of the Body of Christ, God the Son brings in God the Spirit as the capacity of the Body of Christ. First, there is the source; then, there is the element; and finally, there is the capacity. The source is God the Father, the element is God the Son, and the capacity is God the Spirit. Actually, the three are just one. Today, in our living and service, apart from this capacity, we can do nothing and can accomplish nothing....As Christians, the whole key to our living and service in the Body of Christ depends on this capacity of the law of the Spirit of life.

Christ is the life element of the Body of Christ, and the Spirit of life is the essence of this element. This essence becomes the law in the Body of Christ, which is the innate ability of the Body of Christ....The mysterious organism of God is fully a matter of Christ being our life. This life is the element of the organic Body of Christ. The essence that comes with this element is the Spirit of life. This Spirit of life as the essence becomes the law in the Body of Christ, which is the innate power of this Body. (*The Mysteries in God's New Testament Economy*, pp. 78-81)

Further Reading: The Mysteries in God's New Testament Economy,
   ch. 4; *A Thorough View of the Body of Christ,* ch. 3

Enlightenment and inspiration: _____

_____

_____

_____

Morning Nourishment

Rom.   For just as in one body we have many members, and
12:4   all the members do not have the same function.

6-8   And having gifts that differ according to the grace
given to us, whether prophecy, *let us prophesy* according to the proportion of faith; or service, *let us be
faithful* in that service; or he who teaches, in that
teaching; or he who exhorts, in that exhortation; he
who gives, in simplicity; he who leads, in diligence; he
who shows mercy, in cheerfulness.

The service of this organism is the corporate, organic service of
the Body of Christ (Rom. 12:4-8). Our living is corporate, and our
service is also corporate. It is like our human body—there is nothing in it that is not corporate. Whether it speaks or moves, it does
so corporately. The same is true with service in the Body of Christ.
Hence, in this service, every member is necessary (1 Cor. 12:14-22).
Moreover, every member functions organically according to his
measure (Eph. 4:16b). Since we are members in the Body of Christ,
we are all necessary, and we all have our function. Once we fulfill
our function in the Body, we have the corporate, organic service.
(*The Mysteries in God's New Testament Economy*, pp. 70-71)

Today's Reading

Furthermore, this service of the organism is the organic service of the New Testament priesthood of the gospel (1 Pet. 2:5, 9).
This service involves the preaching of the gospel for the saving
of sinners, offering them up as sacrifices to God (Rom. 15:16).
Following that, there is the nourishing of the believers and
helping them to grow so that they can offer themselves up as
living sacrifices to God (John 21:15; 1 Pet. 2:2; Rom. 12:1). In
addition, there is the perfecting of the saints that they may do
the work of the ministry unto the organic building up of the
Body of Christ (Eph. 4:11-16). In addition, we have to lead the
saints to prophesy, to speak for God, for the organic building up
of the church (1 Cor. 14:1, 3-5, 12, 24, 31). These are the four
steps in the practice of the new way....Hence, we all have to be

like the apostle Paul, who labored and struggled in all wisdom to present every man full-grown in Christ to God (Col. 1:28-29). This is the organic service of the Body of Christ. It is for everybody, and it is in a priesthood.

In the organism of the Triune God, whether it be the living or the service, whether it be the growth or the building, everything is organic and must be organic.

Galatians 2:20 says, "I am crucified with Christ, and it is no longer I who live." Our old man, the first husband (Rom. 7:2), has been crucified (Rom. 6:6). We do not belong to ourselves or live to the law anymore. We have become the wife of Christ and have become those who depend on Christ. Hence, it is no longer we who live. We should cease from all our struggling and striving. When we stop and let go of whatever we are holding on to, it is no longer we who live. Following that, in our living or our service, we go along spontaneously with the operation of the law of the Spirit of life in us, cooperating with it. Then the two, that is, the law and us, act as one man, the outward being in harmony with the inward (Gal. 5:16a, 25). We are neither working alone nor are we giving up working altogether. Rather, we are cooperating with the law of the Spirit of life within, fulfilling the demand of this law, going along with the operation of this law within, and spontaneously developing the capacity of this law. For this, we need to cooperate by prayer and by having a spirit of dependence, thus maintaining our fellowship with the Lord of life and the Lord of work (1 Thes. 5:17; Eph. 6:17-18). When we continue to live in the fellowship with this Lord, who is the Spirit of life within us and the law in the Body of Christ, we will have the genuine living and service of the Body of Christ. This will enable us to grow in life, to be filled with the gifts of life, and to develop the organic functions for the building up of the Body of Christ unto the fulfillment of God's New Testament economy. (*The Mysteries in God's New Testament Economy,* pp. 71, 83)

Further Reading: A Thorough View of the Body of Christ, ch. 4

Enlightenment and inspiration: _____

_____

_____

_____

Hymns, #824

1 The Church is Christ's own Body,
　 The Father's dwelling-place,
　 The gathering of the called ones,
　 God blended with man's race;
　 Elect before creation,
　　 Redeemed by Calv'ry's death,
　 Her character and standing
　　 Of heaven, not of earth.

2 New man of new creation,
　　 Born through her risen Lord,
　 Baptized in God the Spirit,
　　 Made holy by His Word;
　 Christ is her life and content,
　　 Himself her glorious Head;
　 She has ascended with Him
　　 O'er all her foes to tread.

3 Christ is her one foundation,
　　 None other man may lay;
　 All that she has, as Christ, is
　　 Divine in every way;
　 Her members through the Spirit
　　 Their death on Calv'ry own;
　 They're built in resurrection—
　　 Gold, silver, precious stone.

4 One God, one Lord, one Spirit—
　　 Her elements all one—
　 One faith, one hope, one baptism,
　　 One Body in the Son;
　 The triune God is in her,
　　 One Body members own,
　 By faith they are united,
　　 In hope of glory shown.

5 From every tribe and nation
　　 Do all the members come,
　 Regardless of their classes
　　 United to be one.
　 No high there is, nor lowly,
　　 No Jew, nor Gentile clan,
　 No free, nor slave, nor master,
　　 But Christ, the "one new man."

6 One Body universal,
      One in each place expressed;
   Locality of dwelling
      Her only ground possessed;
   Administration local,
      Each answ'ring to the Lord;
   Communion universal,
      Upheld in one accord.

7 Her local gatherings model
      The New Jerusalem;
   Its aspects and its details
      Must show in all of them.
   Christ is the Lamp that shineth,
      With God within, the Light;
   They are the lampstands bearing
      His glorious Image bright.

Composition for prophecy with main point and sub-points: _____

_____

_____

_____

_____

_____

_____

_____

_____

_____

_____

_____

_____

_____

_____

_____

_____

_____

_____

_____

Reading Schedule for the Recovery Version of the Old Testament with Footnotes

Wk.	Lord's Day	Monday	Tuesday	Wednesday	Thursday	Friday	Saturday
1	☐ Gen 1:1-5	☐ 1:6-23	☐ 1:24-31	☐ 2:1-9	☐ 2:10-25	☐ 3:1-13	☐ 3:14-24
2	☐ 4:1-26	☐ 5:1-32	☐ 6:1-22	☐ 7:1—8:3	☐ 8:4-22	☐ 9:1-29	☐ 10:1-32
3	☐ 11:1-32	☐ 12:1-20	☐ 13:1-18	☐ 14:1-24	☐ 15:1-21	☐ 16:1-16	☐ 17:1-27
4	☐ 18:1-33	☐ 19:1-38	☐ 20:1-18	☐ 21:1-34	☐ 22:1-24	☐ 23:1—24:27	☐ 24:28-67
5	☐ 25:1-34	☐ 26:1-35	☐ 27:1-46	☐ 28:1-22	☐ 29:1-35	☐ 30:1-43	☐ 31:1-55
6	☐ 32:1-32	☐ 33:1—34:31	☐ 35:1-29	☐ 36:1-43	☐ 37:1-36	☐ 38:1—39:23	☐ 40:1—41:13
7	☐ 41:14-57	☐ 42:1-38	☐ 43:1-34	☐ 44:1-34	☐ 45:1-28	☐ 46:1-34	☐ 47:1-31
8	☐ 48:1-22	☐ 49:1-15	☐ 49:16-33	☐ 50:1-26	☐ Exo 1:1-22	☐ 2:1-25	☐ 3:1-22
9	☐ 4:1-31	☐ 5:1-23	☐ 6:1-30	☐ 7:1-25	☐ 8:1-32	☐ 9:1-35	☐ 10:1-29
10	☐ 11:1-10	☐ 12:1-14	☐ 12:15-36	☐ 12:37-51	☐ 13:1-22	☐ 14:1-31	☐ 15:1-27
11	☐ 16:1-36	☐ 17:1-16	☐ 18:1-27	☐ 19:1-25	☐ 20:1-26	☐ 21:1-36	☐ 22:1-31
12	☐ 23:1-33	☐ 24:1-18	☐ 25:1-22	☐ 25:23-40	☐ 26:1-14	☐ 26:15-37	☐ 27:1-21
13	☐ 28:1-21	☐ 28:22-43	☐ 29:1-21	☐ 29:22-46	☐ 30:1-10	☐ 30:11-38	☐ 31:1-17
14	☐ 31:18—32:35	☐ 33:1-23	☐ 34:1-35	☐ 35:1-35	☐ 36:1-38	☐ 37:1-29	☐ 38:1-31
15	☐ 39:1-43	☐ 40:1-38	☐ Lev 1:1-17	☐ 2:1-16	☐ 3:1-17	☐ 4:1-35	☐ 5:1-19
16	☐ 6:1-30	☐ 7:1-38	☐ 8:1-36	☐ 9:1-24	☐ 10:1-20	☐ 11:1-47	☐ 12:1-8
17	☐ 13:1-28	☐ 13:29-59	☐ 14:1-18	☐ 14:19-32	☐ 14:33-57	☐ 15:1-33	☐ 16:1-17
18	☐ 16:18-34	☐ 17:1-16	☐ 18:1-30	☐ 19:1-37	☐ 20:1-27	☐ 21:1-24	☐ 22:1-33
19	☐ 23:1-22	☐ 23:23-44	☐ 24:1-23	☐ 25:1-23	☐ 25:24-55	☐ 26:1-24	☐ 26:25-46
20	☐ 27:1-34	☐ Num 1:1-54	☐ 2:1-34	☐ 3:1-51	☐ 4:1-49	☐ 5:1-31	☐ 6:1-27
21	☐ 7:1-41	☐ 7:42-88	☐ 7:89—8:26	☐ 9:1-23	☐ 10:1-36	☐ 11:1-35	☐ 12:1—13:33
22	☐ 14:1-45	☐ 15:1-41	☐ 16:1-50	☐ 17:1—18:7	☐ 18:8-32	☐ 19:1-22	☐ 20:1-29
23	☐ 21:1-35	☐ 22:1-41	☐ 23:1-30	☐ 24:1-25	☐ 25:1-18	☐ 26:1-65	☐ 27:1-23
24	☐ 28:1-31	☐ 29:1-40	☐ 30:1—31:24	☐ 31:25-54	☐ 32:1-42	☐ 33:1-56	☐ 34:1-29
25	☐ 35:1-34	☐ 36:1-13	☐ Deut 1:1-46	☐ 2:1-37	☐ 3:1-29	☐ 4:1-49	☐ 5:1-33
26	☐ 6:1—7:26	☐ 8:1-20	☐ 9:1-29	☐ 10:1-22	☐ 11:1-32	☐ 12:1-32	☐ 13:1—14:21

Reading Schedule for the Recovery Version of the Old Testament with Footnotes

Wk.	Lord's Day	Monday	Tuesday	Wednesday	Thursday	Friday	Saturday
27	☐ 14:22—15:23	☐ 16:1-22	☐ 17:1—18:8	☐ 18:9—19:21	☐ 20:1—21:17	☐ 21:18—22:30	☐ 23:1-25
28	☐ 24:1-22	☐ 25:1-19	☐ 26:1-19	☐ 27:1-26	☐ 28:1-68	☐ 29:1-29	☐ 30:1—31:29
29	☐ 31:30—32:52	☐ 33:1-29	☐ 34:1-12	☐ Josh 1:1-18	☐ 2:1-24	☐ 3:1-17	☐ 4:1-24
30	☐ 5:1-15	☐ 6:1-27	☐ 7:1-26	☐ 8:1-35	☐ 9:1-27	☐ 10:1-43	☐ 11:1—12:24
31	☐ 13:1-33	☐ 14:1—15:63	☐ 16:1—18:28	☐ 19:1-51	☐ 20:1—21:45	☐ 22:1-34	☐ 23:1—24:33
32	☐ Judg 1:1-36	☐ 2:1-23	☐ 3:1-31	☐ 4:1-24	☐ 5:1-31	☐ 6:1-40	☐ 7:1-25
33	☐ 8:1-35	☐ 9:1-57	☐ 10:1—11:40	☐ 12:1—13:25	☐ 14:1—15:20	☐ 16:1-31	☐ 17:1—18:31
34	☐ 19:1-30	☐ 20:1-48	☐ 21:1-25	☐ Ruth 1:1-22	☐ 2:1-23	☐ 3:1-18	☐ 4:1-22
35	☐ 1 Sam 1:1-28	☐ 2:1-36	☐ 3:1—4:22	☐ 5:1—6:21	☐ 7:1—8:22	☐ 9:1-27	☐ 10:1—11:15
36	☐ 12:1—13:23	☐ 14:1-52	☐ 15:1-35	☐ 16:1-23	☐ 17:1-58	☐ 18:1-30	☐ 19:1-24
37	☐ 20:1-42	☐ 21:1—22:23	☐ 23:1—24:22	☐ 25:1-44	☐ 26:1-25	☐ 27:1—28:25	☐ 29:1—30:31
38	☐ 31:1-13	☐ 2 Sam 1:1-27	☐ 2:1-32	☐ 3:1-39	☐ 4:1—5:25	☐ 6:1-23	☐ 7:1-29
39	☐ 8:1—9:13	☐ 10:1—11:27	☐ 12:1-31	☐ 13:1-39	☐ 14:1-33	☐ 15:1—16:23	☐ 17:1—18:33
40	☐ 19:1-43	☐ 20:1—21:22	☐ 22:1-51	☐ 23:1-39	☐ 24:1-25	☐ 1 Kings 1:1-19	☐ 1:20-53
41	☐ 2:1-46	☐ 3:1-28	☐ 4:1-34	☐ 5:1—6:38	☐ 7:1-22	☐ 7:23-51	☐ 8:1-36
42	☐ 8:37-66	☐ 9:1-28	☐ 10:1-29	☐ 11:1-43	☐ 12:1-33	☐ 13:1-34	☐ 14:1-31
43	☐ 15:1-34	☐ 16:1—17:24	☐ 18:1-46	☐ 19:1-21	☐ 20:1-43	☐ 21:1—22:53	☐ 2 Kings 1:1-18
44	☐ 2:1—3:27	☐ 4:1-44	☐ 5:1—6:33	☐ 7:1-20	☐ 8:1-29	☐ 9:1-37	☐ 10:1-36
45	☐ 11:1—12:21	☐ 13:1—14:29	☐ 15:1-38	☐ 16:1-20	☐ 17:1-41	☐ 18:1-37	☐ 19:1-37
46	☐ 20:1—21:26	☐ 22:1-20	☐ 23:1-37	☐ 24:1—25:30	☐ 1 Chron 1:1-54	☐ 2:1—3:24	☐ 4:1—5:26
47	☐ 6:1-81	☐ 7:1-40	☐ 8:1-40	☐ 9:1-44	☐ 10:1—11:47	☐ 12:1-40	☐ 13:1—14:17
48	☐ 15:1—16:43	☐ 17:1-27	☐ 18:1—19:19	☐ 20:1—21:30	☐ 22:1—23:32	☐ 24:1—25:31	☐ 26:1-32
49	☐ 27:1-34	☐ 28:1—29:30	☐ 2 Chron 1:1-17	☐ 2:1—3:17	☐ 4:1—5:14	☐ 6:1-42	☐ 7:1—8:18
50	☐ 9:1—10:19	☐ 11:1—12:16	☐ 13:1—15:19	☐ 16:1—17:19	☐ 18:1—19:11	☐ 20:1-37	☐ 21:1—22:12
51	☐ 23:1—24:27	☐ 25:1—26:23	☐ 27:1—28:27	☐ 29:1-36	☐ 30:1—31:21	☐ 32:1-33	☐ 33:1—34:33
52	☐ 35:1—36:23	☐ Ezra 1:1-11	☐ 2:1-70	☐ 3:1—4:24	☐ 5:1—6:22	☐ 7:1-28	☐ 8:1-36

Reading Schedule for the Recovery Version of the Old Testament with Footnotes

Wk.	Lord's Day	Monday	Tuesday	Wednesday	Thursday	Friday	Saturday
53	☐ 9:1—10:44	☐ Neh 1:1-11	☐ 2:1—3:32	☐ 4:1—5:19	☐ 6:1-19	☐ 7:1-73	☐ 8:1-18
54	☐ 9:1-20	☐ 9:21-38	☐ 10:1—11:36	☐ 12:1-47	☐ 13:1-31	☐ Esth 1:1-22	☐ 2:1—3:15
55	☐ 4:1—5:14	☐ 6:1—7:10	☐ 8:1-17	☐ 9:1—10:3	☐ Job 1:1-22	☐ 2:1—3:26	☐ 4:1—5:27
56	☐ 6:1—7:21	☐ 8:1—9:35	☐ 10:1—11:20	☐ 12:1—13:28	☐ 14:1—15:35	☐ 16:1—17:16	☐ 18:1—19:29
57	☐ 20:1—21:34	☐ 22:1—23:17	☐ 24:1—25:6	☐ 26:1—27:23	☐ 28:1—29:25	☐ 30:1—31:40	☐ 32:1—33:33
58	☐ 34:1—35:16	☐ 36:1-33	☐ 37:1-24	☐ 38:1-41	☐ 39:1-30	☐ 40:1-24	☐ 41:1-34
59	☐ 42:1-17	☐ Psa 1:1-6	☐ 2:1—3:8	☐ 4:1—6:10	☐ 7:1—8:9	☐ 9:1—10:18	☐ 11:1—15:5
60	☐ 16:1—17:15	☐ 18:1-50	☐ 19:1—21:13	☐ 22:1-31	☐ 23:1—24:10	☐ 25:1—27:14	☐ 28:1—30:12
61	☐ 31:1—32:11	☐ 33:1—34:22	☐ 35:1—36:12	☐ 37:1-40	☐ 38:1—39:13	☐ 40:1—41:13	☐ 42:1—43:5
62	☐ 44:1-26	☐ 45:1-17	☐ 46:1—48:14	☐ 49:1—50:23	☐ 51:1—52:9	☐ 53:1—55:23	☐ 56:1—58:11
63	☐ 59:1—61:8	☐ 62:1—64:10	☐ 65:1—67:7	☐ 68:1-35	☐ 69:1—70:5	☐ 71:1—72:20	☐ 73:1—74:23
64	☐ 75:1—77:20	☐ 78:1-72	☐ 79:1—81:16	☐ 82:1—84:12	☐ 85:1—87:7	☐ 88:1—89:52	☐ 90:1—91:16
65	☐ 92:1—94:23	☐ 95:1—97:12	☐ 98:1—101:8	☐ 102:1—103:22	☐ 104:1—105:45	☐ 106:1-48	☐ 107:1-43
66	☐ 108:1—109:31	☐ 110:1—112:10	☐ 113:1—115:18	☐ 116:1—118:29	☐ 119:1-32	☐ 119:33-72	☐ 119:73-120
67	☐ 119:121-176	☐ 120:1—124:8	☐ 125:1—128:6	☐ 129:1—132:18	☐ 133:1—135:21	☐ 136:1—138:8	☐ 139:1—140:13
68	☐ 141:1—144:15	☐ 145:1—147:20	☐ 148:1—150:6	☐ Prov 1:1-33	☐ 2:1—3:35	☐ 4:1—5:23	☐ 6:1-35
69	☐ 7:1—8:36	☐ 9:1—10:32	☐ 11:1—12:28	☐ 13:1—14:35	☐ 15:1-33	☐ 16:1-33	☐ 17:1-28
70	☐ 18:1-24	☐ 19:1—20:30	☐ 21:1—22:29	☐ 23:1-35	☐ 24:1—25:28	☐ 26:1—27:27	☐ 28:1—29:27
71	☐ 30:1-33	☐ 31:1-31	☐ Eccl 1:1-18	☐ 2:1—3:22	☐ 4:1—5:20	☐ 6:1—7:29	☐ 8:1—9:18
72	☐ 10:1—11:10	☐ 12:1-14	☐ S.S 1:1-8	☐ 1:9-17	☐ 2:1-17	☐ 3:1-11	☐ 4:1-8
73	☐ 4:9-16	☐ 5:1-16	☐ 6:1-13	☐ 7:1-13	☐ 8:1-14	☐ Isa 1:1-11	☐ 1:12-31
74	☐ 2:1-22	☐ 3:1-26	☐ 4:1-6	☐ 5:1-30	☐ 6:1-13	☐ 7:1-25	☐ 8:1-22
75	☐ 9:1-21	☐ 10:1-34	☐ 11:1—12:6	☐ 13:1-22	☐ 14:1-14	☐ 14:15-32	☐ 15:1—16:14
76	☐ 17:1—18:7	☐ 19:1-25	☐ 20:1—21:17	☐ 22:1-25	☐ 23:1-18	☐ 24:1-23	☐ 25:1-12
77	☐ 26:1-:21	☐ 27:1-13	☐ 28:1-29	☐ 29:1-24	☐ 30:1-33	☐ 31:1—32:20	☐ 33:1-24
78	☐ 34:1-17	☐ 35:1-10	☐ 36:1-22	☐ 37:1-38	☐ 38:1—39:8	☐ 40:1-31	☐ 41:1-29

Reading Schedule for the Recovery Version of the Old Testament with Footnotes

Wk.	Lord's Day	Monday	Tuesday	Wednesday	Thursday	Friday	Saturday
79	☐ 42:1-25	☐ 43:1-28	☐ 44:1-28	☐ 45:1-25	☐ 46:1-13	☐ 47:1-15	☐ 48:1-22
80	☐ 49:1-13	☐ 49:14-26	☐ 50:1—51:23	☐ 52:1-15	☐ 53:1-12	☐ 54:1-17	☐ 55:1-13
81	☐ 56:1-12	☐ 57:1-21	☐ 58:1-14	☐ 59:1-21	☐ 60:1-22	☐ 61:1-11	☐ 62:1-12
82	☐ 63:1-19	☐ 64:1-12	☐ 65:1-25	☐ 66:1-24	☐ Jer 1:1-19	☐ 2:1-19	☐ 2:20-37
83	☐ 3:1-25	☐ 4:1-31	☐ 5:1-31	☐ 6:1-30	☐ 7:1-34	☐ 8:1-22	☐ 9:1-26
84	☐ 10:1-25	☐ 11:1—12:17	☐ 13:1-27	☐ 14:1-22	☐ 15:1-21	☐ 16:1—17:27	☐ 18:1-23
85	☐ 19:1—20:18	☐ 21:1—22:30	☐ 23:1-40	☐ 24:1—25:38	☐ 26:1—27:22	☐ 28:1—29:32	☐ 30:1-24
86	☐ 31:1-23	☐ 31:24-40	☐ 32:1-44	☐ 33:1-26	☐ 34:1-22	☐ 35:1-19	☐ 36:1-32
87	☐ 37:1-21	☐ 38:1-28	☐ 39:1—40:16	☐ 41:1—42:22	☐ 43:1—44:30	☐ 45:1—46:28	☐ 47:1—48:16
88	☐ 48:17-47	☐ 49:1-22	☐ 49:23-39	☐ 50:1-27	☐ 50:28-46	☐ 51:1-27	☐ 51:28-64
89	☐ 52:1-34	☐ Lam 1:1-22	☐ 2:1-22	☐ 3:1-39	☐ 3:40-66	☐ 4:1-22	☐ 5:1-22
90	☐ Ezek 1:1-14	☐ 1:15-28	☐ 2:1—3:27	☐ 4:1—5:17	☐ 6:1—7:27	☐ 8:1—9:11	☐ 10:1—11:25
91	☐ 12:1—13:23	☐ 14:1—15:8	☐ 16:1-63	☐ 17:1—18:32	☐ 19:1-14	☐ 20:1-49	☐ 21:1-32
92	☐ 22:1-31	☐ 23:1-49	☐ 24:1-27	☐ 25:1—26:21	☐ 27:1-36	☐ 28:1-26	☐ 29:1—30:26
93	☐ 31:1—32:32	☐ 33:1-33	☐ 34:1-31	☐ 35:1—36:21	☐ 36:22-38	☐ 37:1-28	☐ 38:1—39:29
94	☐ 40:1-27	☐ 40:28-49	☐ 41:1-26	☐ 42:1—43:27	☐ 44:1-31	☐ 45:1-25	☐ 46:1-24
95	☐ 47:1-23	☐ 48:1-35	☐ Dan 1:1-21	☐ 2:1-30	☐ 2:31-49	☐ 3:1-30	☐ 4:1-37
96	☐ 5:1-31	☐ 6:1-28	☐ 7:1-12	☐ 7:13-28	☐ 8:1-27	☐ 9:1-27	☐ 10:1-21
97	☐ 11:1-22	☐ 11:23-45	☐ 12:1-13	☐ Hosea 1:1-11	☐ 2:1-23	☐ 3:1—4:19	☐ 5:1-15
98	☐ 6:1-11	☐ 7:1-16	☐ 8:1-14	☐ 9:1-17	☐ 10:1-15	☐ 11:1-12	☐ 12:1-14
99	☐ 13:1—14:9	☐ Joel 1:1-20	☐ 2:1-16	☐ 2:17-32	☐ 3:1-21	☐ Amos 1:1-15	☐ 2:1-16
00	☐ 3:1-15	☐ 4:1—5:27	☐ 6:1—7:17	☐ 8:1—9:15	☐ Obad 1-21	☐ Jonah 1:1-17	☐ 2:1—4:11
01	☐ Micah 1:1-16	☐ 2:1—3:12	☐ 4:1—5:15	☐ 6:1—7:20	☐ Nahum 1:1-15	☐ 2:1—3:19	☐ Hab 1:1-17
02	☐ 2:1-20	☐ 3:1-19	☐ Zeph 1:1-18	☐ 2:1-15	☐ 3:1-20	☐ Hag 1:1-15	☐ 2:1-23
03	☐ Zech 1:1-21	☐ 2:1-13	☐ 3:1-10	☐ 4:1-14	☐ 5:1—6:15	☐ 7:1—8:23	☐ 9:1-17
04	☐ 10:1—11:17	☐ 12:1—13:9	☐ 14:1-21	☐ Mal 1:1-14	☐ 2:1-17	☐ 3:1-18	☐ 4:1-6

Reading Schedule for the Recovery Version of the New Testament with Footnotes

Wk.	Lord's Day	Monday	Tuesday	Wednesday	Thursday	Friday	Saturday
1	Matt 1:1-2	1:3-7	1:8-17	1:18-25	2:1-23	3:1-6	3:7-17
2	4:1-11	4:12-25	5:1-4	5:5-12	5:13-20	5:21-26	5:27-48
3	6:1-8	6:9-18	6:19-34	7:1-12	7:13-29	8:1-13	8:14-22
4	8:23-34	9:1-13	9:14-17	9:18-34	9:35—10:5	10:6-25	10:26-42
5	11:1-15	11:16-30	12:1-14	12:15-32	12:33-42	12:43—13:2	13:3-12
6	13:13-30	13:31-43	13:44-58	14:1-13	14:14-21	14:22-36	15:1-20
7	15:21-31	15:32-39	16:1-12	16:13-20	16:21-28	17:1-13	17:14-27
8	18:1-14	18:15-22	18:23-35	19:1-15	19:16-30	20:1-16	20:17-34
9	21:1-11	21:12-22	21:23-32	21:33-46	22:1-22	22:23-33	22:34-46
10	23:1-12	23:13-39	24:1-14	24:15-31	24:32-51	25:1-13	25:14-30
11	25:31-46	26:1-16	26:17-35	26:36-46	26:47-64	26:65-75	27:1-26
12	27:27-44	27:45-56	27:57—28:15	28:16-20	Mark 1:1	1:2-6	1:7-13
13	1:14-28	1:29-45	2:1-12	2:13-28	3:1-19	3:20-35	4:1-25
14	4:26-41	5:1-20	5:21-43	6:1-29	6:30-56	7:1-23	7:24-37
15	8:1-26	8:27—9:1	9:2-29	9:30-50	10:1-16	10:17-34	10:35-52
16	11:1-16	11:17-33	12:1-27	12:28-44	13:1-13	13:14-37	14:1-26
17	14:27-52	14:53-72	15:1-15	15:16-47	16:1-8	16:9-20	Luke 1:1-4
18	1:5-25	1:26-46	1:47-56	1:57-80	2:1-8	2:9-20	2:21-39
19	2:40-52	3:1-20	3:21-38	4:1-13	4:14-30	4:31-44	5:1-26
20	5:27—6:16	6:17-38	6:39-49	7:1-17	7:18-23	7:24-35	7:36-50
21	8:1-15	8:16-25	8:26-39	8:40-56	9:1-17	9:18-26	9:27-36
22	9:37-50	9:51-62	10:1-11	10:12-24	10:25-37	10:38-42	11:1-13
23	11:14-26	11:27-36	11:37-54	12:1-12	12:13-21	12:22-34	12:35-48
24	12:49-59	13:1-9	13:10-17	13:18-30	13:31—14:6	14:7-14	14:15-24
25	14:25-35	15:1-10	15:11-21	15:22-32	16:1-13	16:14-22	16:23-31
26	17:1-19	17:20-37	18:1-14	18:15-30	18:31-43	19:1-10	19:11-27

Reading Schedule for the Recovery Version of the New Testament with Footnotes

Wk.	Lord's Day	Monday	Tuesday	Wednesday	Thursday	Friday	Saturday
27	☐ Luke 19:28-48	☐ 20:1-19	☐ 20:20-38	☐ 20:39—21:4	☐ 21:5-27	☐ 21:28-38	☐ 22:1-20
28	☐ 22:21-38	☐ 22:39-54	☐ 22:55-71	☐ 23:1-43	☐ 23:44-56	☐ 24:1-12	☐ 24:13-35
29	☐ 24:36-53	☐ John 1:1-13	☐ 1:14-18	☐ 1:19-34	☐ 1:35-51	☐ 2:1-11	☐ 2:12-22
30	☐ 2:23—3:13	☐ 3:14-21	☐ 3:22-36	☐ 4:1-14	☐ 4:15-26	☐ 4:27-42	☐ 4:43-54
31	☐ 5:1-16	☐ 5:17-30	☐ 5:31-47	☐ 6:1-15	☐ 6:16-31	☐ 6:32-51	☐ 6:52-71
32	☐ 7:1-9	☐ 7:10-24	☐ 7:25-36	☐ 7:37-52	☐ 7:53—8:11	☐ 8:12-27	☐ 8:28-44
33	☐ 8:45-59	☐ 9:1-13	☐ 9:14-34	☐ 9:35—10:9	☐ 10:10-30	☐ 10:31—11:4	☐ 11:5-22
34	☐ 11:23-40	☐ 11:41-57	☐ 12:1-11	☐ 12:12-24	☐ 12:25-36	☐ 12:37-50	☐ 13:1-11
35	☐ 13:12-30	☐ 13:31-38	☐ 14:1-6	☐ 14:7-20	☐ 14:21-31	☐ 15:1-11	☐ 15:12-27
36	☐ 16:1-15	☐ 16:16-33	☐ 17:1-5	☐ 17:6-13	☐ 17:14-24	☐ 17:25—18:11	☐ 18:12-27
37	☐ 18:28-40	☐ 19:1-16	☐ 19:17-30	☐ 19:31-42	☐ 20:1-13	☐ 20:14-18	☐ 20:19-22
38	☐ 20:23-31	☐ 21:1-14	☐ 21:15-22	☐ 21:23-25	☐ Acts 1:1-8	☐ 1:9-14	☐ 1:15-26
39	☐ 2:1-13	☐ 2:14-21	☐ 2:22-36	☐ 2:37-41	☐ 2:42-47	☐ 3:1-18	☐ 3:19—4:22
40	☐ 4:23-37	☐ 5:1-16	☐ 5:17-32	☐ 5:33-42	☐ 6:1—7:1	☐ 7:2-29	☐ 7:30-60
41	☐ 8:1-13	☐ 8:14-25	☐ 8:26-40	☐ 9:1-19	☐ 9:20-43	☐ 10:1-16	☐ 10:17-33
42	☐ 10:34-48	☐ 11:1-18	☐ 11:19-30	☐ 12:1-25	☐ 13:1-12	☐ 13:13-43	☐ 13:44—14:5
43	☐ 14:6-28	☐ 15:1-12	☐ 15:13-34	☐ 15:35—16:5	☐ 16:6-18	☐ 16:19-40	☐ 17:1-18
44	☐ 17:19-34	☐ 18:1-17	☐ 18:18-28	☐ 19:1-20	☐ 19:21-41	☐ 20:1-12	☐ 20:13-38
45	☐ 21:1-14	☐ 21:15-26	☐ 21:27-40	☐ 22:1-21	☐ 22:22-29	☐ 22:30—23:11	☐ 23:12-15
46	☐ 23:16-30	☐ 23:31—24:21	☐ 24:22—25:5	☐ 25:6-27	☐ 26:1-13	☐ 26:14-32	☐ 27:1-26
47	☐ 27:27—28:10	☐ 28:11-22	☐ 28:23-31	☐ Rom 1:1-2	☐ 1:3-7	☐ 1:8-17	☐ 1:18-25
48	☐ 1:26—2:10	☐ 2:11-29	☐ 3:1-20	☐ 3:21-31	☐ 4:1-12	☐ 4:13-25	☐ 5:1-11
49	☐ 5:12-17	☐ 5:18—6:5	☐ 6:6-11	☐ 6:12-23	☐ 7:1-12	☐ 7:13-25	☐ 8:1-2
50	☐ 8:3-6	☐ 8:7-13	☐ 8:14-25	☐ 8:26-39	☐ 9:1-18	☐ 9:19—10:3	☐ 10:4-15
51	☐ 10:16—11:10	☐ 11:11-22	☐ 11:23-36	☐ 12:1-3	☐ 12:4-21	☐ 13:1-14	☐ 14:1-12
52	☐ 14:13-23	☐ 15:1-13	☐ 15:14-33	☐ 16:1-5	☐ 16:6-24	☐ 16:25-27	☐ 1 Cor 1:1-4

Reading Schedule for the Recovery Version of the New Testament with Footnotes

Wk.	Lord's Day	Monday	Tuesday	Wednesday	Thursday	Friday	Saturday
53	1 Cor 1:5-9	1:10-17	1:18-31	2:1-5	2:6-10	2:11-16	3:1-9
54	3:10-13	3:14-23	4:1-9	4:10-21	5:1-13	6:1-11	6:12-20
55	7:1-16	7:17-24	7:25-40	8:1-13	9:1-15	9:16-27	10:1-4
56	10:5-13	10:14-33	11:1-6	11:7-16	11:17-26	11:27-34	12:1-11
57	12:12-22	12:23-31	13:1-13	14:1-12	14:13-25	14:26-33	14:34-40
58	15:1-19	15:20-28	15:29-34	15:35-49	15:50-58	16:1-9	16:10-24
59	2 Cor 1:1-4	1:5-14	1:15-22	1:23—2:11	2:12-17	3:1-6	3:7-11
60	3:12-18	4:1-6	4:7-12	4:13-18	5:1-8	5:9-15	5:16-21
61	6:1-13	6:14—7:4	7:5-16	8:1-15	8:16-24	9:1-15	10:1-6
62	10:7-18	11:1-15	11:16-33	12:1-10	12:11-21	13:1-10	13:11-14
63	Gal 1:1-5	1:6-14	1:15-24	2:1-13	2:14-21	3:1-4	3:5-14
64	3:15-22	3:23-29	4:1-7	4:8-20	4:21-31	5:1-12	5:13-21
65	5:22-26	6:1-10	6:11-15	6:16-18	Eph 1:1-3	1:4-6	1:7-10
66	1:11-14	1:15-18	1:19-23	2:1-5	2:6-10	2:11-14	2:15-18
67	2:19-22	3:1-7	3:8-13	3:14-18	3:19-21	4:1-4	4:5-10
68	4:11-16	4:17-24	4:25-32	5:1-10	5:11-21	5:22-26	5:27-33
69	6:1-9	6:10-14	6:15-18	6:19-24	Phil 1:1-7	1:8-18	1:19-26
70	1:27—2:4	2:5-11	2:12-16	2:17-30	3:1-6	3:7-11	3:12-16
71	3:17-21	4:1-9	4:10-23	Col 1:1-8	1:9-13	1:14-23	1:24-29
72	2:1-7	2:8-15	2:16-23	3:1-4	3:5-15	3:16-25	4:1-18
73	1 Thes 1:1-3	1:4-10	2:1-12	2:13—3:5	3:6-13	4:1-10	4:11—5:11
74	5:12-28	2 Thes 1:1-12	2:1-17	3:1-18	1 Tim 1:1-2	1:3-4	1:5-14
75	1:15-20	2:1-7	2:8-15	3:1-13	3:14—4:5	4:6-16	5:1-25
76	6:1-10	6:11-21	2 Tim 1:1-10	1:11-18	2:1-15	2:16-26	3:1-13
77	3:14—4:8	4:9-22	Titus 1:1-4	1:5-16	2:1-15	3:1-8	3:9-15
78	Philem 1:1-11	1:12-25	Heb 1:1-2	1:3-5	1:6-14	2:1-9	2:10-18